LIFE'S TOUGHEST LESSONS
AREN'T MEANT FOR NOTHING

by Terry Dodd

**God is *always* to be trusted,
even if we don't understand.**

Copyright © 2007 by Terry Dodd

LIFE'S TOUGHEST LESSONS Aren't Meant For Nothing
by Terry Dodd

Printed in the United States of America

ISBN 978-1-60266-568-2

All rights reserved solely by the author. The author guarantees all contents are original and do not infringe upon the legal rights of any other person or work. No part of this book may be reproduced in any form without the permission of the author. The views expressed in this book are not necessarily those of the publisher.

Unless otherwise indicated, Bible quotations are taken from the New International Version of the Bible. Joint copyright © 1995 by Tyndale House Publishers, Inc. and Zondervan Publishing House.

www.xulonpress.com

TABLE OF CONTENTS

Part I:
Trial by Journey 19

Fire In The Hole 21
Why Me, Lord? 23
Where Is God's Love? 25
School Of Affliction 27
Judy's Genesis 29
Good, But Unsaved 31
Quiet Witness 33
Punishment Or Pruning? 35
Wandering 37
Mountaintop Experience 40

The Word Revealed 43
The Plot Engages 44
Surrender 47
First Fruit 51
Symphony Of Love 53
Marriage Enriched 55
Retirement 57
The News 59
Life Resumes 64
Winds Of Change 67

Tribulation 70
Strength Through Him 72
Plans A, B, & C 74
Doubling Up 76
Repeating Our Vows 78
Praise And Prayer 80
Hospitalized 82
What Cheer! 84
Hope Springs From The
    Heart 86
Lessons Come Faster 88

Witnessing Of A Different
    Sort 91
Ministry Working 93
Familial Love And Support 95
What Is Man? 97
Dreaded Planning 99
The Joy Of Witnessing 101
The Privilege Of Being
    Helped 103
Thumbs Up 106
What Keeps Us Keepin'
    On? 109
Onward, Christian Soldiers 113

v

Strength To Comfort Others 116	A Hard Lesson 190
Sharing 118	Home And Heart 192
By The Grace Of God 121	
What Awaits Me After Death? 123	Death Is Not The End Of Life 195
Three Not Of A Kind 127	Christ's First Coming Merely Interesting? 197
It's All About Trust 129	Attitude Itself A Witness 200
Sweet Sounds 131	The Real Meaning Of Marriage 202
Earn, Save, Give, Pray 134	
Life Lines 136	The Joy of Simple Things 204
Iowa Comes To Georgia 138	It's Not About Me 206
	Hope Abounds 210
Faithful Friends 140	For The Love Of God 213
Abundant Blessings 143	Time Becomes More Precious 215
Enter Hospice 147	
Joking Around 150	Transforming Truths 218
What Limits, Forgiveness? .. 152	
A Special Christmas 155	This Is Your Life 221
The Hope That We Have In Christ 157	The Struggle Intensifies 222
	Fore! 225
Love God, Love People 159	Why Did God Make Me? 227
I Will Have Mercy On Whom I Have Mercy 161	Love Shines Through 230
	Shutting Down 233
Man's Hell-Bent Rebellion 164	The Dying Experience 235
	Gone From My Sight 237
God's Grace 166	Preparing Ourselves 238
Spreading One's Joy 168	Saved From What? 239
Squirrels Fly And Books Speak 172	
	Judy's Call 240
Holy Cabinet And Paper Cups 175	Honoring A Promise 242
	Finding Our Way 244
Rejoicing Through One's Trials 177	Is There A Cure? 246
	September Song 248
The Power Of Prayer 181	Readiness 249
Believe-It-Or-Not 184	Nearer Thy God 252
Putting On A Happy Face 187	Final Day 255

Part II:
Journeying Alone 259

Life Ahead.............................260
Sunday's New Day................262
Symphony Revisited 264
Re-gathering..........................266
Change In Crises 268
God Closes One Door/Opens
    Another 270

Part III:
A New Journey 273

A New Day..............................274
Coming To Grips....................277
Full Circle 279
Changing Lanes 280
How Not To Begin A
    Relationship 284
Helga's Genesis.....................287
Misfortune In Marriage........289
Healing Helga 290
Road To Recovery.................292
Ode To Spiritual Intimacy 294

With A Song In My Heart 296
Revelation 299
Bullet Summary 302
Rejoicing In The New Day 304
Closure 306

AUTHOR'S NOTES & ACKNOWLEDGMENTS

In capsule form, this is what I believe: Christians are not born; they are born again. No one is a Christian because of lineage, heritage or parentage. Individuals become Christians when they realize they are sinners with no way of removing their sins, they believe that Jesus willingly accepted the punishment they deserve, and they commit their lives into His loving care.

I am thankful for the grace of God in that so many lessons–through both trial and blessing—have fallen upon me in the course of my life. This book is intended to be a personal testimonial to the importance of putting one's full trust in the Lord, regardless of circumstances.

By framing some of these lessons out of the extensive personal journal entries I made over nearly a two year period between 2004 and 2006 I have tried to share the hope we all have in Christ through the good–and especially the bad–times in our lives. I believe the tough lessons in life are truly meant for good. As much as we struggle with this when we are most burdened by loss and trauma, God's plan–in which He promises to prosper us so that we can produce more fruit for His kingdom—does not change. After all, for what purpose were we made? To know God.

I give most of the credit for my inspiration in writing this book to the memory of my beloved late wife, Judy, about whom this narrative is primarily written. It is only through God's prevenient grace that I came to accept Jesus Christ as my Lord and Savior—however late in life. And it is through Him that Judy and I and the love of our 46 years of marriage were so richly blessed. Those blessings brought with it three loving children, their wonderful spouses, and our precious grandchildren, all of whom had their own special roles in the inspiration of this writing.

God also made special provision for aiding my recovery from the trauma of my loss of Judy through my new wife and helper, Helga, and her family. Helga's love for me, her participation with me in our various ministries, and her encouragement of this book have been the glue of my own new days. A friend wrote to me recently to say that many people do not have the blessing of one loving spouse in their lifetime, but that I have been blessed through two marriages with wonderful, loving women. I continue to be amazed at how much God yet blesses sinners such as you and me.

And while God allows–and sometimes even causes—calamity in our lives, it always–somehow–has a purpose. That life's difficult lessons are anything but easy is a gross understatement, but we simply cannot know God's ways. Certainly, neither you nor I *want* tragedy in our lives, but God is *always* to be trusted, whether or not we understand. People are watching us as we stay at our post, alertly, unswervingly . . . immersed in tears, yet always filled with deep joy.

I owe a special debt of gratitude to Wayne Clark, who offered many valuable suggestions to the manuscript. His input not only helped to keep me focused, but also provided some critical Scriptural understanding. To Pat Anderson, many thanks, not only for her dedicated proofing, but for the lesson that an author who relies upon himself to proof his work has a fool for a proofreader. And I owe special appreciation to Jay Hill and Gloria Overvold for their undertaking to read an unfinished manuscript and provide me with penned endorsements.

The single greatest lesson I have learned in life is that I–like you– was made to search for God. What a tremendous gift to know — absolutely — that if we search for Him in earnest He *will* make Himself known (Isaiah 55:6 and Hebrews 11:6). Thank you, Lord, for softly calling to me.

Terry Dodd

Other Books Authored by Terry Dodd

Uncommon Influence. This is a gripping business/science fiction novel of the power of advertising, and of those who would use it in a devious struggle for control of the minds of others. The only novel ever published set in the uniquely personal advertising medium known as promotional products.

"Just when you think you've got the story figured out, a new twist develops . . . like a hall of mirrors."
–Bobby Bowden, Head Football Coach, Florida State University

250 pages, 6" x 9" paperback, $14.95. Out of print, but with limited availability through amazon.com.

Ultimate Encounter. This stand-alone sequel to *Uncommon Influence* is a fast-paced Christian science fiction novel. Its theme evolves from the real life UFO enigma and the quest for reciprocal communication with UFO occupants. Whether or not UFOs and their supposed occupants represent a benign curiosity or a sinister presence, God remains universal, for there cannot be competing Creators.

"Start with a highly imaginative story line, add one part Robert Ludlum, a measure of Gene Roddenberry, and a pinch of Mickey Spillane. Then, bring it all to a boil through the sure-handed pen

of a veteran Christian author, and that's as close as I can come to describing Terry Dodd's latest book."
–David Hubbell, M.D., Emory University School of Medicine

270 pages, 6" x 9" paperback, $16.95. Available through www.pleasantword.com

The Foursome. A compelling and compassionate Christian novel set against the background of a casual golf match among four strangers. During the game the players are felled by lightning, yet the match miraculously continues. With eternal life itself on the line one man's faith is matched against doubt, ignorance, and pride.

"I could not help but be convicted by the parallels between my human struggles in golf and my very personal relationship with the Lord."
–Chris Cupit, Rivermont Golf Club Manager

350 pages, 5 ½" x 8" paperback, $16.95. Available through www.selahpublishing.com

Foreword

The Bible tells us that God is sovereign. That means He either causes or allows all things. So what do we do with pain and suffering in our lives? Whom do we blame? If we try to protect God from blame, we wind up creating a second prime being (Satan) as the author of evil and suffering. This leaves the high ground to God but it is dualism and then God is NOT sovereign. Or we can take the position that "stuff happens" and that is fatalism. Again it leaves the high ground to God but He is, once again, no longer sovereign.

God is not the author of evil. All evil is caused by the abuse of man's free will. But God clearly causes or allows calamity, suffering, difficulty and pain. He says so. In Isaiah 45:6-7 He tells us:

> There is no one besides Me.
> I am the LORD, and there is no other,
> The one forming light and creating darkness,
> Causing well-being and creating calamity;
> I am the LORD who does all these. NAS

Before we judge God too harshly let us remember that, as loving parents, we are like that ourselves. We cause or allow calamity, suffering, difficulty and pain in the lives of our beloved children. We do it because we think it is good for them and that without it they will not grow. We do it because we know that to spare them from it or rescue them too often from it will create an even greater calamity, suffering, difficulty or pain in their lives over time. How do we do that, you say? We make them get stitches when they fall and cut themselves, in spite of their protestations that, "This is bad!" We make them go to school in the face of plaintive wailings that they want to stay home with mommy. We put the aging and suffering house pet down even though our children may tell us we are cruel, even murderous. From their young, limited and narrow point of view, these things are calamitous–causing them suffering, difficulty and pain.

Jesus twice tells us that we need to trust that God is a good Father who would not give his child a snake if the child asked for a fish. He would not give us a rock if we asked for a piece of bread. He would not give us a scorpion if we asked for an egg. We need to give God credit for being at least as loving, caring and wise as we are with our own children. We need to trust Him (for that is the foundation of faith-based relationships). Even though it sometimes seems hard as a rock, that trust is bread, and even though it sometimes wriggles and hisses, it is as fish (Lk 11:9-13; Mt 7:7-11).

My wife and I did not learn this in a book. In 1994, I suffered a permanent paralysis of my diaphragm. In 1999, we lost our 17-year old as well as my father within five months' time. In 2004 I had two cancers, three surgeries, radiation therapy and other physical issues. We have lost money and jobs, and friends have been disillusioned by the things of this world, but we have never lost hope or joy through any of this. We have been the beneficiary of a great grace. God has met us in the furnace when He did not keep us out of it. We have had a "peace that passes understanding" because we have been the beneficiary of good biblical teaching and a sound biblical theology concerning the sovereignty of God and how He meets us (even prospers us) in our difficulties.

Over the centuries God has revealed important truths to certain men and women for the benefit of us all. He showed Marconi the principles of the radio, Edison the light bulb, Alexander Graham Bell the telephone, George Washington Carver over 200 uses for the peanut, Sir Isaac Newton the principles of gravity, and Madame Curie the uses and benefits of penicillin. All of these individuals were seeking God's truth and looking for it where it was not likely to be found. They had no evidence of its existence, only a belief that a good God would have provided it. From their trust flowed their belief. From their belief flowed their actions. From their actions flowed their discovery of truth.

God will reveal important truths to us all when we seek Him, and sometimes "accidentally" even when we do not. Many of those truths are discovered by ordinary people in extraordinary circumstances when they meet difficulty with faith. Trusting in a loving and sovereign God, they find a "peace that passes understanding" in the most trying and difficult times. They look beyond what is seen and comprehend what is unseen but, nonetheless, real. They can see beauty beyond the ugliness, gain beyond the loss, benefit beyond the difficulty and life after death. Because they see it, really see it, because it is revealed to them who really seek it, they act on it and thereby reveal it to others who are observing their struggle. They are witnesses to a truth they see but which we cannot see until we see it in them. Then it can become revealed to us if we will only allow ourselves to see and understand.

Two such people are Terry and Judy Dodd. What they both suffered in Judy's terminal cancer and the way they handled it is a look into the divine realm. Their willingness to share and Terry's gift of writing enable us to look upon the most intimate learning experiences of their lives. Based on daily journalings over more than nineteen months, Terry reveals to us a process that is both fresh in its pain and powerful in its telling. This is not whitewashed retelling. It is open heart surgery, as intimate and personal as it gets. Although Terry attempts to be apologetic when he can, he mostly just tells us a love story about two people who, based in God, find peace, strength and even joy in the most devastating of circumstances. Terry does not try to overwhelm us with his logic. He just makes claims and gives testimony with such authority that the reader knows that it is true.

Ultimately, the story reveals a loving Father in Heaven who wants nothing but the best for His children and who knows that sometimes the best requires exercise and stretching to strengthen, develop, grow and mature them. So, although He mostly provides pleasant things for them to experience, His parental wisdom also allows them to have difficulty, to suffer pain and even to die that they might achieve the highest of joys, pleasures and understandings. Terry and Judy show us that God is a Father we can trust to love us, to provide for us and also to develop us, to mature us and to allow us to overcome great obstacles that we might become great saints. In Hebrews 11:35-40, people like Terry and Judy are called "men and women of whom the world is not worthy." And these, having gained approval through their faith, were in this manner being perfected.

Wayne Clark

Setting the Stage for *Life's Toughest Lessons*

Of this manuscript—before it became a book—a friend described its pages as "a window into two lives in difficulty." This isn't so much a story about my losing Judy to cancer, however, as it is about our responses to her condition. And while this life *is* a terminal condition for all of us, death is not the end of life.

In the process of describing the events seen through this "window" and how they impacted the two of us, this testimony often references "pruning." To some, the use of this gardener's term may be confusing, but I use it in the context of how God works to ultimately benefit us. In other words, pruning here refers not to the radical lopping or cutting off of superfluous branches, but rather to God's shaping, perfecting and refining people such that they can produce more fruit for His Kingdom.

Part 1: Trial by Journey

FIRE IN THE HOLE

Over dinner on November 7, 2005—only six weeks after the love of 46 years of my life crossed over—I sat at the dinner table in Jacksonville, Florida with my daughter Wendi, son-in-law Kevin, and Messianic Rabbi David Levine and his wife Sandy. We had been discussing both the concept and the actual losses of loved ones, and the struggles of those left behind. I shared with everyone at that time some notes I had made in my Bible on August 23, 1998, a little over seven years prior to my late wife, Judy's, passing.

At the time of my note-taking I had been reading from the third chapter (verse 16) of the Book of Daniel. There we read that King Nebuchadnezzar was furious with Shadrach, Meshack and Abednego as they responded to his threat that they could either do as he bid them and worship the ninety foot high image of gold he had constructed, or be thrown into a blazing furnace. Nebuchadnazzar added, "Then what God will be able to rescue you from my hand?"

The reply that came from the God-fearing threesome was this: "If we are thrown into the blazing furnace, the God we serve is able to save us from it , and he will rescue us from your hand, O king. But even if he does not, we want you to know, O king, that we will not serve your gods or worship the image of gold you have set up."

My point is not that of their incredible bravery–which was certainly the case. Rather it is that, even though old King Neb then made good on his threat, the three acted quite literally in "good faith" in spite of knowing what might well happen. They understood that if God *always* rescued those who were true to him, believers would not need faith. In other words, as the venerable NIV translation points out, if that were all it took to be saved; i.e., intellectual knowledge, their religion would merely be a great insurance policy, and there would be lines of selfish people ready to sign up to *supposedly* serve God if they knew absolutely that He could be counted on to intervene in their behalf. Big deal. Even the demons know the Truth of Christ, but they are not saved.

Believers in Jesus Christ as their Lord and Savior serve for the love of God, for the love of our Creator. In this serving we, the created, come to understand Christ's breathtaking promise that death is not the end of life. Most people live under the assumption that life is the sum total of time between one's birth and physical death, rather than from birth to everlasting life. The Bible tells us something quite different.

Each of us must deal with the tough lessons that life deals us. God is God, and He will have mercy upon whom He will have mercy. And though we may not understand, we must learn to live with our shortcomings. Such lessons as these, however, are not meant for nothing. Without them we would not be capable of producing the very fruit for which God has both created and refined us.

This book has been written out of my personal inspiration as to why and how one can place all of one's trust and hope in our living God. That said, it is important to make it clear that if I own any degree of righteousness it must be attributed to God's mercy and not to my own merit. The fact is that I am–just as are you—deeply flawed, but the Lord works to give us an obedient heart. I pray for this very thing. And though we are saved by grace I fully embrace God's will for believers that we yet need to finish this life in repentance, setting ourselves apart from the world and dedicated to what we understand is God's vision for our lives.

WHY ME, LORD?

Martin Luther said, "He who is able to learn, therefore let him learn, in order that when afflicted and assailed everyone may conclude that the world, the devil, death, and misfortune are only God's hoe and clipper; that all the revilement and disgrace the Christian experiences is God's way of fertilizing him."

One of the saddest but most common refrains heard by those dealing with tragedy is, "Why me, Lord?" In my case I don't know exactly why God sent me my personal cross of such excruciating emotional pain over the loss of Judy, but I neither questioned him then nor do I now. Others do, and that is certainly okay. But isn't it interesting when the question of "why" is asked—though it is usually intended to be rhetorical–it is nevertheless usually directed at God? I suppose this is so because it is difficult to understand that God knows best in everything and in every matter. Though at the time of deep hurt through a personal tragedy, it is often well beyond an individual's comprehension that His word remains: "In all things God works for the good of those who love Him, who have been called according to His purpose" (Romans 8:28).

Okay, you've probably heard that before. Yet you may question how you are to buy into such a Scripture in what appears/appeared to be the darkest hour of your life. Consider this: the event is God's intervention to preserve us from something even more severe. Judy did not belong to me or to our children. She belonged to God. In wanting Judy's life spared I asked God on more than one occasion essentially the same question Jesus asked in the Garden of

Gethsemane: "Lord, if there be another way, may it be granted. Yet not as I will, but as You will."

We are told in Scripture that the trials God permits in the believer's life are designed to make us more steadfast and confident in relying wholly on Christ. Now, I know what many will think in reaction to this, as in, "Give me a break!" After all, the concept of a life of obedience and complete dependence is not easily grasped, let alone realized. Even the apostle Paul of the New Testament found this concept to be precisely the case until by the grace of God he matured in his thinking. He tells us of the actual change in his thinking in Philippians 4:12: "I have learned the secret of being content in any and every situation."

Yes, I know this flies in the face of what the world teaches. When I was seven years old I was caught up in a leaf fire in foolhardily attempting to jump over it. My right pant leg caught fire. The Lord gave me the presence of mind to remove my coat, cover the leg with it, and roll on the ground in order to smother the flames. There were serious consequences to my foolishness, however. The skin of my entire right leg–from the ankle to the knee–was burned to ash. Today, when I touch that wonderfully scarred leg it feels different than my other leg. There will always be a great scar. A tough lesson in life is like that. The loss is permanent and we will never be the same, but we cannot profitably wallow in our self-pity.

You may have experienced the loss of a spouse, parent, child, or other deeply loved one. Or perhaps you have suffered some other traumatic life's event such as divorce, loss of a job, a serious accident or lingering illness (either on your part or that of a loved one). Unfortunately, if you haven't already suffered one or more of these, you surely will. But take heart, for time will stretch the pain for you, as it has for me. The bad news–at least in the case of loss of a loved one — is that even after months, a year, five, ten or more years, an image or a memory will still touch the scar. The good news is that the intensity should be lessened and the scar will be touched less frequently. In other words, without diminishing the need for a reasonable amount of time to mourn one's loss, survival nevertheless requires adjusting to both reality and new circumstances.

WHERE IS GOD'S LOVE?

Lessons in dealing with life's toughest times aren't limited to the actual tragedies themselves. They just as often come from learning about God's purpose for us. Understandably, some people ask where the love of God is for a believer who puts all of his or her trust in Him and who yet continues to suffer the afflictions of a terminal disease, a divorce or other life tragedy. Is God's love evident even though His physical healing seems to be absent? Where is the love of God when others seem compelled to say, "Look to your own ways, for God is not there?" Would anyone expect another to boast only of God when to the unbelieving eye, ear, and heart not only is God not everywhere, but He is *no*where?

Exactly how does one perceive God's presence? Is He "here" because He answers a specific prayer in a specific fashion? Is He "there" because others have attributed His presence to their prayers being attended? Is He "everywhere" because those who call upon Him say He is?

Allow me to submit a few personal examples of how one would recognize both God's presence and His love. Judy would awaken each new dawn from her night of "sleep," sitting in an armchair with her head tilted either forward or to one side, and her words to me as she looked out her window at our front yard were, "It's another beautiful morning." That's God's love.

Many times, in the middle of the night she would find herself even shorter of breath than normal and would have to fight her impulse to hyperventilate in order to draw more life-sustaining oxygen. I would caress her arms and head, and in response she would say, "You're my comfort, but you're supposed to be asleep." Her repetitious use of "you" rather than "I" perfectly reflects God's love.

When the two of us would step onto an elevator on the way to a doctor's appointment and Judy would say to a complete stranger, "That's a pretty blouse," and the woman would respond in both surprise and appreciation with, "Why, thank you," that is God's love.

When Judy's oncologist came into the examination room to assess her condition but instantly laughed out loud to see her portable oxygen tank dressed as a little girl; and then before he could turn to leave afterward she asked him abut his children, especially the one who had just started her first job as a pastor, well . . . that is God's love.

When family rallied around Judy, and friends from our church offered not only their hands to cook but their hearts in prayer, that is God's love. And when many of those same hands and hearts picked up a pen to write out a check to help with an impossibly expensive medical treatment not covered by Medicare or secondary insurance, is that not God's love at work?

When God allowed us enough time together in life so that Judy and I were permitted to get off the road and into retirement before cancer could claim its hold on her body, what else would support such spiritual positiveness except His love?

And, finally, consider this example. A longtime friend—now passed on—sent us a note in response to Judy's offer of a computer we weren't using, along with a thank you for his love and support. He wrote: "I just don't know people like you. With all your problems, you think of others. Whatever you have is very special. I am honored to have friends like you." To my friend Bob I could only reply, "What we have is God's love."

What is it God wants from us? He wants neither our promises nor our good intentions. He doesn't even want our Christian service. What He wants is *us*. As pastor/author Steve McVey puts it, "Everything else takes care of itself when we just rest in His arms, allowing Him to act through us." If God didn't love us would He have sent His only Son away from His eternal seat beside the Father in order to come to earth in the form of a man to die for us?

SCHOOL OF AFFLICTION

God has so many lessons to teach us that He must run many schools. The most effective of these may be the school of affliction, for without suffering we would know nothing of sympathy. As the noted Dr. J. Allen Blair puts it, "The heart that has never ached under the strain of a tremendous burden has never discovered the meaning of understanding."

Many people become embittered and cynical, yet through implicit trust in our Lord Jesus Christ, we come to recognize that new dimensions have been added to our lives. Again, we turn to the apostle Paul and his dealing with what he termed his "thorn in the flesh." Three times he prayed to God, seeking divine removal of the thorn, whether his "thorn" was weeping eyes and poor vision (from being blinded on the road to Damascus) or something else. How did God answer? "My grace is sufficient for you, for my power is made perfect in weakness." How's that? Consider that weakness develops character and, more importantly, it deepens our worship of God, because in admitting our weakness, we affirm God's strength.

Paul's thorn remained, but God gave Paul all-sufficient grace to live with his thorn. In fact, as Dr. Blair points out, because of Paul's devotedness to Christ, the thorn became beauty, the heartache became joy, and the misery was mastered. Never was Paul's usefulness hindered or his service ineffective because of the thorn. Though he suffered greatly in his pursuit of obedience to the Lord, his attitude was, "most gladly therefore will I rather glory in my infirmities that the power of Christ may rest upon me."

Judy made ample use of her time to reflect upon the things of eternity and those things that are truly important. She prayed that God's will be done in her life. She did not love God any less for not healing her. She knew that His grace was sufficient for her. Billy Graham puts it this way: "Earth's troubles fade in the light of heaven's hope."

As for me, Paul's confidence in trusting in the Lord in all things—which means neither to worry nor fret–gave me peace in joyously caring for Judy through the cancer that ultimately took her life. And as for my own thorns in the flesh (minor ones, mind you) I have found that once I quit complaining about them and praying for God to remove them, each became totally manageable. God is probably telling me that I am better off not being in perfect health, so that I more fully appreciate my dependence upon Him.

JUDY'S GENESIS

Judy K. Dodd (born Judith Carol Kingery) was only five years old when she first turned to God for love and counsel. An awareness of her need for Him was born out of the first of a number of childhood sexual molestation events made worse by the disbelief of those who should have protected her. Her maternal grandmother, however—correctly understanding her need—gave little Judy her first biblical lesson, one which would serve her through a lifetime.

Grandmother Campbell held her granddaughter close to her as she patiently and tenderly explained that not only did she have a Father in heaven who loved her, but that she could also talk to Him at any time about any thing. Did she understand? From that day forward Judy took her fears, her questions, her prayers, her praises and her hopes to the Father on a regular basis.

As she was finishing her schooling and continuing to mature in her faith, early on I picked her out from the sea of nearly 600 senior high school students in a small town in central Iowa. As we later began to date and then find that our joy in being with one another was love, we also had wonderful conversations about a hoped-for marriage and the raising of a family. We talked about how we would do some things differently than our parents and some things we would copy. What we didn't talk about was our individual relationships with Jesus Christ.

While my parents maintained a regular church connection for the family, I had no true relationship with God. While I don't recall my parents ever discussing with me either the concept of salvation or their own faith in Christ, I do vividly recall not wanting to hear my father's talk about "the birds and the bees." At the latter announcement I covered my ears and dove under a chair while my 21-month younger brother waved off our father with, "I know all that!" In truth, I may have turned such a deaf ear to any talk of the Lord, but I certainly do not recall it.

Merely holding a Bible while sitting in a church pew doesn't make one a believer in Jesus Christ as Lord and Savior any more than holding a hammer makes one a carpenter. What would you say defines one's relationship with God? When I say that as a child I regularly attended Sunday School and church but had no relationship with the Lord, I mean I did not pray privately. And as my church's senior pastor puts it, " Prayer *is* one's relationship with God."

Contrast my circumstances at the time with Judy's. She had a strong personal relationship with Him although her family was *not* churched. Nevertheless, she often found a way attend a particular church service or activity with friends. Her faith was held closely to her heart and mind. Interestingly, she did not initially passionately share with others her abiding faith, even with me as we began to date. Since I had no saving faith of my own I certainly did not bring up the subject, other than to boast of my perfect Sunday School attendance.

GOOD, BUT UNSAVED

This yoking of our unequal-but-loving relationship would continue through our late-teen romance and into our marriage at age twenty and well beyond. In fact, for the nearly forty (yes, forty) years to follow I don't recall a single time of seriously broaching the subject of faith with Judy. She taught our children to pray, which I only lamely encouraged. On rare occasion I did provide a means—but not active encouragement—for our children to attend Sunday School or church. In other words my spiritual leadership of the family was absent. I was a dutiful and loving, good and ethical husband and father. But that does not get one into heaven. I had not been saved from God's wrath at a sinful people who choose to follow their own paths rather than that given to us through the sacrificial blood of Christ. Neither had I truly begun to understand the concept of sacrificial love.

As a child I was baptized and later confirmed in that baptism. From the ages of eight through eighteen I earned more perfect attendance pins than anyone in my church's age group. Through all of those years and the forty years to follow, however, I never learned the single most important lesson of them all. I never, ever had a personal relationship with the Lord and Savior of the world. Righteousness–not works–is what has the power to save someone. That's what saved Abraham and Moses, even though they did not have the benefit of the gospels as we do.

I did not understand–or, perhaps, simply refused to dwell on its meaning–the teaching that Christ left the side of God the Father to come to earth in the form of man and bring us the message that the only way to salvation is through a relationship with Him. He did this for me and He did it for you. God's Word tells us this is so. The saddest commentary of life on earth today is how few of us heed His message. I was as stubborn in this respect as anyone I know. And I think this is a very descriptive term—stubbornness—for I nor anyone can claim ignorance.

My parents unfailingly sent me to Sunday School, and on occasion, took themselves and we boys to church. I do not recall, however, having even one family discussion concerning the importance of a personal relationship with Christ. As children, my two brothers and I were taught to pray rote prayers before every meal and at bedtime, but as important as prayer is, if it is merely a prayer for prayer's sake and fails to evoke any sense of either personality or dependance, then prayer is nothing but an exercise and will be quickly abandoned.

I wanted to be like my father. He was my model in life, family, business and sport. Yet, when he died—six years before I came to Christ—neither he nor I nor my two brothers could console either him or ourselves in prayer. I wanted to be like him with respect to his success as a husband and father, with respect to his business career, and especially with respect to his ability to get up and down in two strokes from anywhere just off the green. I can't blame him for my failure in the latter category. And I certainly don't want to blame my parents for my own apostasy, yet the sins of the fathers are visited upon the sons to three and four generations. But one cannot hide either behind or in spite of his upbringing forever. Man is without excuse. Not only is the evidence for God all around us, but His word is in nearly every home in America. However close I might have been to learning that lesson in my adolescence, I fell far away from it immediately upon graduating high school.

QUIET WITNESS

Judy, on the other hand, continued her youthful personal prayer life into adulthood. Her witness to me at the time we began dating came not in the form of her telling, but in her actions. It wasn't until many years later that I not only came to learn about her childhood difficulties, but also that she had prayed for me from the start of our relationship.

In November 1998, only two years after having accepted Christ, I took a weekend Christian retreat called Walk to Emmaus. It was during that walk that I deposited at the foot of the cross the remaining baggage I had continued to carry even after having come to Christ. As I emotionally shared with those on the retreat, and then with Judy and my youngest son, Martin, upon my return, the Walk was–and still has been—the single most meaningful three-day period of my entire life. The following is excerpted from Judy's letter to me which I read on the final day of my Walk:

"To My Dear Terry: I have loved you from our second date some forty-two years ago. In my prayers I have always thanked God for letting us meet, fall in love and stay in love all these years. I love you with all of my heart and will forever and beyond. I am glad God gave you to me to love and share my life."

Wow! And what a loaded last sentence. "I am glad God *gave* you to me." God makes it easy to find Him and it is through His prevenient grace (that grace which God gives us before we know Him) that He knew I would ultimately seek Him. Up until a specific point in time, however, I had never bothered looking in His direction, let alone being interested in His offer. I shudder to think that I might easily have waited too long to establish a saving relationship. After all, tomorrow is given to no man. Up until the age of 58, the circumstances of which I will share after a few more pages, I knew *of* Him, but I did not *know* Him.

In the Old Testament this word "know" means more than the mere knowledge of the Lord. After all, countless people have Bibles in their homes and thus "know" of God the Father and even of God the Son and God the Holy Spirit. But they will have no excuse on judgement day if they do not repent (change their ways) and believe. Even demons know of the Father, but they do not believe. Biblical "knowing" implies an intimate relationship with God. Again, I did not know Him, whereas Judy had known Him since the age of five.

Jesus puts it to us as simply as possible. Matthew 11:27 reads: "All things have been committed to me by my Father. No one knows the Son except the Father, and no one knows the Father except the Son *and those to whom the Son chooses to reveal to Him"* (emphasis mine). In other words, for anyone else to know God, God must reveal Himself to that person, by the Son's choice. How blessed was I that Jesus revealed Himself to me so late in life. Had I not sought Him, however, that would not have happened.

It is my personal belief that the Holy Spirit descended upon Judy at an incredibly truly tender age and never deserted her. You may feel that this is quite a statement, if true. What's my authority for making such a claim, for certainly no one in the Old Testament had the Holy Spirit continuously. The God Christians know did not become incarnate until the appearance of Jesus Christ; that is, when God's Word became a human being. When He entered the human condition He committed Himself to suffer and die. But what happened next to Jesus the Christ is that He took the world's evil into Himself. He rose again, so that those who have faith in Him will enter a realm where every tear will be dried and the problem of evil will disappear. Little Judy gained that faith and never gave it up. And when she died, her faith allowed her to enter, healed, into the everlasting realm of the Father.

PUNISHMENT OR PRUNING?

Judy and I were so in love early in our lives together, as well as at the end. I left home in the Fall of 1957, upon high school graduation, to enter military service for two years. In those times this was common. Many fathers thought enlistment the best solution to the otherwise inevitable drafting of young men at about age 22. This obviously made it more difficult for Judy and me to continue the development of a normal boy-girl relationship. At our mutual age of 19, however, we tearfully and reluctantly gave each other permission to date others. Neither of us did. When I came home during Christmas leave only three months later I brought with me a special gift for her. It had cost me an entire month's pay. The gift of that $78 dress in today's inflated economics would be something on the order of $1,500!

The "gift," purchased in the most fashionable dress shop in downtown Augusta, Georgia, was a form-fitting and beautiful blue-sequined dress with a matching blue chiffon top. The shimmering garment would later become known in family legend as The Dress, and was even displayed on a mannequin at Judy's funeral visitation. Unfortunately, it was several sizes too small for her classic hourglass figure, yet her mother and her two sisters managed to pour her into the dress. I loved her in it, partly because, as my daughter Wendi now likes to put it, "she was barely in it." The dress was subsequently handed down to our daughter, and more recently to our granddaughter, Abigail, who is eagerly waiting to grow into it.

Those days, and the many years to follow, were certainly wonderful ones. My toughest lessons in life were still to come.

The Christmas following my presentation of The Dress I proposed marriage to the delight of my eyes. In late March of 1959—six months before I would be honorably discharged from active duty with the U.S. Army—we married and began our lives together, I to be her protector and she to become the human inspiration of my soul.

WANDERING

Between March of 1959 and Christmas of 1996 we lived successively, in Texas, Iowa, Florida, Wisconsin, Iowa once again, Ohio, and finally, Georgia. During that time Judy delivered our three healthy and happy babies, one at a time. Except for a few months in Iowa during 1970 and again in Ohio in 1978, I don't recall actually taking any of our children to either Sunday School or church, or even encouraging them to otherwise attend. Our daughter, however, chose to attend anyway, tagging along with friends, just as her mother had done before her. Spiritually, I was wandering far out in the desert.

Did my college education and its four-plus years enlighten me in the least as to the ways of the Lord? Hardly. In fact, I recall one particular discussion with my best friend at Florida State University in Tallahassee during my senior year. We agreed that what was important in understanding the universe was a solid understanding of the role of the geological and biological evolution of land and man.

While I was doing well in every other part of my studies I was struggling with a single course involving spatial relationships. When I was about to receive a grade of "D" in structural geology—the notice of which I learned only a week before graduation exercises—the head of the geology department called me into his office.

He told me that a grade of less than "C" in one's major would not permit FSU's awarding of a degree, my overall three-point-barely grade point average notwithstanding. Fear struck me with the implications of that statement. Intuitively, I went on the offense. I said,

"Look, Doctor DeVore, I'm going into sales in a field totally unrelated to geology. Surely you can cut me some slack on this matter."

After taking several moments to absorb my input, he intoned gravely, "Son, here's what I can do. If you promise *never* to enter the field of geology, I'll waive the requirement." Well, my mother and father raised no fools (although my very late-in-life coming to Christ could easily have belied that statement). My relieved response was short and to the point: "Where do I sign?"

As I have said, not only did I not know Christ at the time, I was not seeking Him. Time wore on. Judy not only provided the family nurturing but continued her unflagging prayer life, both for our children and for me. She did so in a meaningful—if quiet witness—fashion. While I willingly accepted the roles of loving husband and father, modest provider, family disciplinarian, general encourager and leader, my leadership did not include trust in the Lord for any thing, much less *all* things.

One of my favorite photographs—which has clung magnetically to my refrigerator for many years— shows our daughter and oldest son, Jason, kneeling side-by-side, eyes closed, hands together and pointed upward as they are praying at bedside. Our daughter was about ten years old at the time and the photo shows her attentiveness. The four-year old, however, is displaying a slight grin on his face as if to say, "This is fun, whatever we're doing." Praying is something they were to learn at their mother's side, not mine.

From an early age Judy had been taught to be non-confrontational, and that lesson (together with the Holy Spirit having descended upon her at an early age, bringing with Him the fruit of the Spirit) manifested itself in an incredibly kind, gentle and caring nature. She took a sincere interest in anyone with whom she had contact. By virtue of her early childhood she could much more easily have been transformed into a bitter, self-indulgent person. But with the Lord's help she both forgave and overcame. She began building spiritual foundations early in life, just as we are admonished in Ecclesiastes 12:1: "Remember your Creator in the days of your youth, *before* the day's of trouble come."

Christ brings profound comfort to believing people in their deepest need because they know that God is with them in their suffering. Perhaps because of Judy's suffering so early in life she was even more able to take hold of God's hand during the times of both her early and later trials, and not complain of her lot, fully able to get her arms around the concept of Paul's contentment with circumstances.

Matthew 5:10 tells us to "rejoice and be glad, for your reward is great in heaven." The epitaph I had engraved on Judy's cremation bench is in keeping with her life. It reads, in a paraphrase from 1 Thessalonians 5:16, "She was joyful always: prayed continually; gave thanks in all circumstances, for this was God's will for her in Christ Jesus." She is certainly remembered for what she did in her lifetime, but even more importantly for who she *was* in her lifetime.

I end this chapter with a comment about something you may be asking yourself: How did God's refining fires benefit Judy, who passed away at what most would say was "before her time?" The simple answer is that I don't know what God has in store for her in His presence, but she knew that all she was required to do was place her complete trust in Him. And that included, quite literally, dying to Him. What I do know about that is if Jesus had not gone to prepare a place for her and would return for her—as well as for all believers in Him, He would have told us. He tells us that very thing.

MOUNTAINTOP EXPERIENCE

The apostle Paul (as Saul) met with what I would call the single most dramatic episode of repentance in man's history. This took place when he encountered the voice of the Messiah on the road to Damascus as this rabinnic Jew was murderously intent upon persecuting Jewish believers in Yeshua (Jesus). Perhaps most people cannot identify a specific moment or event in association with their salvation, but others have had their own mini-version of Paul's Damascus-road conversion. Paul's experience came as in a light so bright that it literally left him blinded for three days. In that process the Lord spoke to him unambiguously: "Saul. Saul. Why are you persecuting me?"

My experience was not nearly so dramatic, but equally compelling. During the Summer of 1996 the Lord began to reveal Himself to me. Without realizing it, I began drawing close to Him. First, I was nudged to investigate the invitation contained within a series of direct-mail pieces we had been receiving from a near-by evangelical church. The message was worded in this fashion: "Instead of watching Elvis re-runs this Saturday night why don't you come and hear about the true King. Come as you are from golf or tennis or from your yard." The mailing piece referred to a new service at the church called Saturday Sabbath service. This was an obvious attempt to reach those who might find it more convenient to attend church on Saturday evening.

One Saturday afternoon, as I was driving home from playing my usual weekend round of golf, something remarkable happened. After several months of having ignored God's repeated beckoning via the church mailings, I resolved to scratch my itch by taking in a one-time church service, although I hadn't selected which Saturday I would do so. As I exited the Rivermont club parking lot I remembered the church invitation to "come as you are." Since it was on my "to do" list, I decided at that moment to make a right turn towards the church instead of the left turn which would take me to my subdivision. At the time I believed I was simply intrigued to see what it was like to set foot inside of a church for the first time in more than twenty years.

As the service proceeded and worship hymns were sung, something amazed me. I actually knew the words to some of them. They were apparently still riveted into my memory from my childhood and adolescent years of Sunday School and church. An even greater surprise came as I left. I had the feeling that I needed to come again, if only to confirm that the strange tugging at my heart was nothing more than heartburn from a golfing mid-round chili-dog.

The following Saturday I repeated both my game of golf and the church visit. This time I found my emotions flooded. I had a vague sense of having come "home." I was both excited and confused. I asked Judy if she would join me in attending church the following Saturday. I had shared with her some of my thoughts about the two church visits. She had been quite surprised by my visits and my comments about them. She was even more surprised at my request for her to attend again with me. She readily agreed, however, without making a big deal over it, and thus perhaps putting too much expectation into things.

I was obviously being drawn to pursue my strange sense of "homecoming." When God chooses us in Him before we are ever born this means He never ceases to softly call us, but it also means we have to receive His choice of us. In other words, we have to choose to believe His Word. Once we do, we are sealed with the Holy Spirit. Does God know whether or not we will choose Him at some point? The Bible says He knows everything, thus He certainly must foreknow, yet we must still choose.

Grace from God manifests itself to mankind in two primary ways. The first is through common grace, that is, he showers general blessings on saved and unsaved alike (Psalm 145:8-9), The second way is special, or saving, grace. In this circumstance God irresistibly works in the mind and heart of a person so that the individual freely chooses to believe in Jesus Christ as Savior.

That next weekend I chose to at least begin regularly attending church. Perhaps it was miraculous, but I had discovered–although I would not have been able to articulate it—what a wonderful experience it was to not only spend time considering the words of God's special revelation to man, but to do so in the company of the person who meant most in the world to me.

THE WORD REVEALED

After only the third successive church visit by the two of us, I went home and dusted off the nearly seven pound Bible I had bought for Judy in 1958 while I was stationed with the U.S. Army at Ft. Sam Houston in San Antonio, Texas. I believe it was the only Bible in our home at the time. The first church staff person we met other than pastors was Valorie. Remember her name for she would play an increasingly larger role in our lives. Judy and I went to visit with her in her office to discuss our interest in joining the church. She was not only encouraging and caring–as we told her something of our stories–but she also prayed with us. That was the first time I had ever been prayed with—in person—as an adult, other than at our wedding.

Oddly enough, all of this was happening at a time when I had just given up on writing the novel I had been working on for over a year. Two years earlier I had determined to write that novel–my second–which was a story which would focus on a fictional golf tale involving a faith-conflicted foursome! Originally, I merely planned the foursome's make-up to be a generally contentious and random group. Then—because I was a religious skeptic myself–it came to me that if the foursome were made up of four passionate but disparate views about both faith and life I would have the makings for an interesting story within the framework of a weekend round of golf.

I thought my need was simply to write. What I didn't realize was that *The Foursome's* subtitle of "one man's faith matched against doubt, ignorance and pride" would essentially be a fictionalized version of parts of my own struggle, and that the idea itself was a seed planted by God. I had finished the first draft but hadn't shared with Judy the subsequent writing block I had developed.

THE PLOT ENGAGES

I had hung a note from the bottom of my computer monitor as a reminder to develop the story through three avenues: 1) character conflict leading to conclusion, 2) its dramatic but economic telling, and 3) developing rememberable characters *not* by descriptions but by actions. Notice I had made no mention of prayer, the Word, faith in the Almighty, or a saving relationship with Jesus Christ. For a story about conflicted faith I was well on the road to ruin.

Having stubbornly gone forward with my woeful research in trying to develop the flawed plot, yet another dubious seed sprouted. This one concerned the make-up of *The Foursome's* characters. I knew enough to easily develop fictional resumes for three of the four players: a strong-willed bad-guy atheist, a light-hearted agnostic, and a religious skeptic (even though I chose to make him Jewish). I hadn't any idea, however, of how to write a resume for my fourth character, a born-again Christian. That was a term which I knew, but with which I neither had a personal reference nor really understood. In order to make the story work I would have to grasp this latter concept. How would I go about coming to such an understanding? If you are wondering why I chose a storyline for which I was so unprepared to develop, so did I. Now, of course, I realize that the seed for the idea did not come from my mind.

A year-long draft had been completed, but then shelved out of frustration at my inability to breathe life into the story. This had all taken place prior to my solo trip to church. Incredibly, my research for the story had basically included general encyclopedic references and a short list of books and references *about* the Judaeo-Christian faith. In 1993 the Internet was not yet a part of my or anyone else's life, or at least of no one I knew personally.

After a full year of 50 nearly successive five-hour Sunday morning writing efforts all I had accomplished was a single sad draft. The reason for this was not obvious to me at the time, other than that I knew I had no feel for the Christian hero. How becalmed was I? If I had had a rudder for my sailboat I could have moved forward, had I some wind at my back.

Then suddenly, a freshening wind appeared out of nowhere. What happened was very strange. Obviously, I realized I hadn't done proper research. But what to do about it? The thought suddenly entered my mind to consider reading through the Bible, strictly as a matter of research. Judy's and my church attendance for several months had no doubt contributed to such a thought. Duh! One day I made a fretful decision to enter a Christian book store for the first time in my life.

I recall that visit very distinctly because in wandering around the store shopping for a Bible I actually feared I might be found out for not being a Christian. Rather meekly, I asked for a recommendation of a translation, quickly paid for a copy of a large-print NIV study Bible, and darted home. I felt fortunate to have escaped without being asked for my spiritual credentials.

I immediately began reading. Not really knowing how or where to begin I began with page one of the Old Testament. It wasn't long before I found myself immersed in the story of Genesis, voraciously reading both the text and the accompanying notes.

I managed to get through Genesis, Exodus, and Leviticus, but bogged down in Numbers. Nervously, but excitedly, I jumped ahead to the New Testament and the Gospels. Barely underway, I was instantly fascinated with Matthew's story. As exciting as Genesis had been, I hadn't realized the connection between parts one and two of the Bible. Where had all of this been hiding? How dense was I to have spent all those years in Sunday School never understanding anything more about man and life than that a mysterious God supposedly existed? What had those stories we read meant to me? Had I been totally disengaged, both mentally and spiritually, during all those Sunday mornings from age 10 through 18? Or was it simply that I truly never understood that a relationship with Jesus meant having a prayer life? All salvation is based in relationship, not on either works or knowledge. Further, all relationship is based in trust. Judy knew that.

I was about to be taught far more meaningful lessons than those which came with wandering without faith for forty years. I had no idea of either the revelation or the pruning that lay in store for me. It would take even more time before I would also understand that the difficult lessons yet to take place in my life were not punishment for my dalliance. And yet I would later be troubled on that very matter. I mean, was it possible God actually took Judy home merely in order to create in me a clean heart? How could I live with that?

SURRENDER

My initial–if only partial—surrender to Him came when I could get no further than early in the book of Matthew, the first book of the Gospel. Understand that for most of the time I was reading the Bible I felt I was merely sailing along in my "research" mode, reading and absorbing useful information for my born-again character and his faith arguments. I believe that whole scenario was a part of God's plan for me. Things suddenly took on a very different perspective, however, when I got to Matthew's chapter ten, verse 33. The preceding lead-in verse (number 32) did not present me with a problem, but verse 33 was patently problematic for the state of my mind. In fact, the verse beached my research boat; and along with it, my heart and mind.

I was reading the words of Christ Jesus Himself as He was preparing His disciples for the persecution they would suffer in His name. Quite suddenly, I felt as if God was speaking directly to me as well. In other words, as I was reading and absorbing that particular passage of the Gospel I believe the Holy Spirit (Jesus' Spirit) descended upon me. I don't mean as in some mystical Hollywood film depiction, but rather in my having an awareness of how insignificant and arrogant I was. I suddenly saw myself as having judged my Creator. By having denied God I was judging Him.

As He flooded my spirit the scales began flying from my eyes. In a single moment I realized that not only had I transgressed mightily for forty years, I needed to ask for God to forgive me, to help me turn away from my former thinking, and to accept Jesus Christ as my Lord and Savior. At age 58 I was ready to accept God's free gift of salvation. I had come close to Him for the first time in my life, prompting Him to come close to me.

The fifteen words which primed me in Matthew 10:32 for the fifteen words to follow—which, in effect, converted me—were these: "Whoever acknowledges me before men, I will also acknowledge him before my Father in heaven." Okay, that was cool. A generous offer. No problem. But then came 10:33, the words which brought me to my knees in surrender: "But whoever disowns me before men, I will disown him before my Father in heaven." Holy smokes!

That was the moment at which my eyes began raining tears. Here is another way of describing what that verse meant to me at that moment: I contemplated the notion of the Creator of the universe—the Maker of man—giving me a very personal thumbs down for my overt denial and disobedience of Him! That realization was numbing to my soul. Anyone who challenges God will come away limping, just as Jacob did when he wrestled with Him at Bethel (Genesis 32: 24-32).

What I had been reading flashed before me in no uncertain understanding. The Father had sent His Son to earth to live among us so that He might sacrifice Himself for our sins and so resurrect Himself and His promise of salvation and eternal life for those who believe. And what had been my lifelong reaction to that incredible gift? Arrogant rejection. Who was I to reject God? My eyes continued to flood at the realization of my grave and stubborn disobedience.

I was a person who clearly understood obedience to my earthly father. During my formative years my father had been my earthly idol. Rarely had I willfully disobeyed him, at least once I had learned that to do so not only earned for me consequences I didn't like, but embarrassment at his disappointment in me. I had always wanted to be like him. The magnitude of discovering my lifelong disobedience to a heavenly Father was overwhelming to me. And yet, through all this the only reason I finally "got it" was through God's grace, not because I had chased down the answer. It takes the Holy Spirit to convict someone. But obviously, I *had* . . . finally . . . sought after Him.

That very day I sat Judy down and emotionally shared with her everything that had been going on with me. I mean, the idea of reading the Bible for research purposes, the anxious purchase of a Bible, the actual reading, and all of my aforementioned thoughts and reactions. How did she take it? She was beside herself with joy! A lifetime of her prayers for me had been answered.

There were other factors that had been at work, however. For instance, there were our daughter and son-in-law's remarkable witnesses in answering questions I had matter-of-factly posed for them from time to time. They wondered about that and what effect such conversations had on me. Both the questions and their answers had fermented in my mind. I now knew I wanted to give my life to Christ.

The time was late Fall, 1996. As Judy and I continued going to church I began spending nearly an hour each early morning devouring His Word and praying for guidance. Then, at the Christmas Day dinner table of that year at our daughter and son-in-law's home in Jacksonville, with my mother and granddaughter present, and Judy at my side and holding my hand, I confessed with my mouth that I had never known Christ but now repented of my sins. Further, I asked for God's forgiveness and for Jesus to come into my heart.

To say the least, I startled everyone present except Judy. Following my prayer, my son-in-law said that day was one of the happiest of his life. My daughter would say that she had always assumed I was walking in faith, but didn't know at what level. Frankly, that was not an easy thing for me to hear. I mean, I was ashamed that it wasn't true. The sails of my becalmed boat, however, had finally caught a bold wind before I could default by drifting into oblivion. I had obviously risked much in waiting so late in life, for man knows not his time.

Within only a few months I committed to following our senior pastor's suggestion to the congregation to read the Bible completely through (both Old and New Testaments). I did so and then repeated that joyous experience again the following year. It was during that course of study that I surrendered even more of myself to Him as I took to heart the four core points of the Gospel message: God loves us; we have sinned; God *still* loves us; we must respond in faith. When much later I thought of how gently God had set about pruning me after 40 years of wandering, I also realized how dense my orchard's untrimmed trees must be. He had only begun perfecting me. What lessons remained in store!

FIRST FRUIT

When I was unregenerated I did as Paul describes in Romans 7. That is, not only did I do the things I shouldn't do, I did not do the things I should do. Interestingly, one of the very first fruits of the "new man" I had become took place almost overnight. During my next game of racquetball—a game I had been regularly playing for nearly fifteen years with my Off the Wall Gang–a dramatic change took place. For all those prior years I had thought nothing of loudly cursing during our highly competitive doubles games. I am embarrassed to say that such cursing included both the use of the "F" word and taking the Lord's name in vain. In fact I was guilty to the point of one particular member of our group's commenting on it on a number of occasions. Bud, a good friend and someone who declared himself to have no belief or interest in the supernatural, nevertheless often took me to task for my profanity.

In fact, using the Lord's name disparagingly had never bothered me on the golf course or the racquetball court, or even whenever my thumb happened to be the recipient of a misdirected hammer blow. I assiduously avoided cursing of any kind, however, in the presence of my wife or children. Why that same conscience-filter didn't seem to work for me in the heat of competition or stress, I have no idea.

Well, my point is that immediately following my conversion I suspended swearing, replacing those cheap vocabulary words with a minor lament of "Phooey!" Like many people, I had either chosen to ignore—or simply never gave a thought to—the fact that God recognizes no excuse for denying Him, i.e., "You shall not take the name of the Lord your God in vain." The second half of that verse, however, really lays it on the line: "For the Lord will not hold him guiltless who takes His name in vain." That lesson stayed with me. In fact, I tried to make up for it in yet another way by incorporating its righteousness into the conscience of my semi-alter ego character, Ben Clayman, in my novel, *The Foursome*.

I have a friend who has a solution to handling a situation on the golf course when someone in his group takes the Lord's name in vain and then belatedly realizes his playing partner is an ordained minister. If the person opts to apologize, my friend's response is to say, "If you aren't concerned with saying it before God you shouldn't be concerned with saying it before me."

On this matter I hear so many people today–especially young adults–casually use the lamentable phrase, "Oh, my God!" As innocent as you might think this phrase, it is my opinion that this clearly violates God's teaching. Why? Profanity can be understood as "common" or "ordinary," in contrast to the word holy, which means "unique, different," or "separate."

In other words, I believe using such a phrase casually and vainly dishonors God's name. Again, I want to qualify my position as personal. One of my good Christian friends who read this unfinished manuscript took direct exception to my position, and another constructively labeled my comments on the subject as "preachy." As you can see I have, nevertheless, left my comments in. One acclaimed Christian author states that God is jealous for His name because to profane His name is to assault His character. We are certainly taught that His name is special. I believe we should at least be careful of using God's name in an exclamatory fashion when we are not addressing Him in faith. Even though I still—on rare occasion—do it myself, I believe it to be wrong.

SYMPHONY OF LOVE

A year later at Christmas I gave Judy a shadow box plaque with a letter that still hangs in my office, in Helga's and my home today. I read it aloud during Judy's memorial service on October 1, 2005. Only weeks before the Christmas of 2000 I had called her into my downstairs office to play for her a song written in the 1940s, entitled *Symphony*. The song spoke to my heart for her. The letter I subsequently wrote to her concerning this song reads as follows:

"To Judy, my Symphony and My Love. The music to this haunting Benny Goodman ballad will forever remind me only of you. The lyrics make me cry with joy for your love and tenderness. I owe you so much for what you have shared with me and our children and grandchild. The Lord has truly blessed me. You are one of the reasons I have accepted salvation through Jesus Christ and see a much clearer need to continue working to find a closer connection to Him:

> Sym-pho-ny, symphony of love.
> Music from above. How does it start?
> You walk in and the song begins. Singing violins start in my heart.
> Then you see, the melody seems to rise.
> Then you sigh, it sighs and it softly dies.
> Sym-pho-ny. Sing to me.
> Then we kiss, and it's clear to me you are my symphony.
> My sym-pho-ny.

I signed it simply, "Terry."

How is all this "growth" related to the difficult lessons in life? That's actually it. From lessons come growth. In the case of believers in Christ, it is called sanctification. Do we grow more from difficult lessons or happy ones? I think the former. And in my case, through personal growth in my love for the Lord I also grew in sensitivity for my wife, both of which served to make my fruit-bearing more productive. God tells us that we *must* produce fruit. Yet, even when we do, He will prune us so we can produce yet more fruit. Further, we are told that if we don't produce fruit at all, we will be cut off, which is a Biblical euphemism for taking someone out!

MARRIAGE ENRICHED

From the day we began going to church services together, participating in small groups, regularly praying (corporately, mutually, and privately), and still later when each of us was led to find ministries of our own, our marriage grew from one of mutual love and happiness to one of much deeper love and joy. This resulted in even greater respect and servanthood for one another as well as an unbounded joy in our mutual trust in and for the love of God. Life became richer for us in every way possible, through family, through our business, through our sensitivity for and relationship with each other. And, of course, it naturally deepened our relationship with our Lord and Savior, Christ Jesus.

Judy's fervent, daily prayers for each of our children; that they would complete their education, find meaningful and rewarding employment, and successfully and happily marry, were all fulfilled by 2002. In 2003 Judy felt called to join the Intercessory Prayer Ministry team at Mt. Pisgah. She began receiving daily e-mailed prayer requests from both Valorie and Mike, who was our Minister of Caring. She developed a caring routine of listing each of the requests in a small book. She would pray for them individually as she entered them, along with those on her permanent prayer list. Beyond that point she would pray for them collectively. This shortly turned into a nightly thirty minute prayer time which she would maintain for the rest of her life, only another three years.

In mid November of 2003 we made a final impending-retirement territory trip together, to the Florida panhandle. I called on customers in Tallahassee and Panama City before we headed East to Jacksonville to visit with KWAK (Kevin, Wendi, Abigail and Karsten). As we drove we sang in celebration of our past lives together, the very day itself, and the many new adventures we anticipated we would be living together.

At Judy's encouragement over the next few days I gave my Christian witness in a devotion at Wendi and Abigail's Elijah home schooling group. In the course of my presentation I juggled three clubs, deliberately dropping some in making my devotional point that God's forgiveness for our ongoing mistakes is so much greater than man's quick judgment. You see how easy it is to build in some theme to cover for an amateur's juggling drops? For Karsten's class, which was studying the letter "J," I juggled four balls while making a similar but simpler case for God's love and forgiveness.

God opposes the proud but gives grace to the humble. For those two momentary devotional events I was the BMOC. That sort of well-intentioned but often misdirected focus by others in attendance—although obviously in a much more profound way—actually happened to John the Baptist as he was proclaiming the coming of the Messiah. For a time, some mistakenly thought he was the One to come. That is, until he clearly pointed out to the crowds that he was not the main feature, that in fact he was not fit to clean the sandals of He who would come.

RETIREMENT

December of 2003 brought several business Christmas parties for Judy and me at which my retirement from forty years in the promotional products industry was recognized. I was given beautiful jade glass bookends—contributed by my largest line, Moderne Glass. This was an award for the local association to present, an association of which I had been made an honorary lifetime member and which I had served as president twenty years earlier. The etched inscription included my name, date of my retirement, grateful acknowledgment of my contributions, and the two earlier-mentioned verses from Matthew: "Whoever acknowledges me before men, I will also acknowledge him before my Father in Heaven. But whoever disowns me before men I will disown him before my Father in Heaven." Following the Christmas dinner I spoke to a mostly secular audience, giving my industry testimonial, honoring Judy, and witnessing for Christ.

The first week in January Judy and I again drove to Jacksonville. It had been a full year since Judy began her prayer warrior ministry. The primary purpose of our trip was for me to meet with Rabbi David Levine and his wife, Sandy, to plan for my own new ministry—a postal newsletter focusing on supporting the Messianic movement and Shalom Network International. This was to be primarily a fundraising responsibility as I was joining SNI as a paid independent contractor, a job for which I not only felt strongly called, but for which I had lobbied. At that time SNI was headquartered in Kiev, Ukraine, founded by the Levines who were friends of ours through our daughter and son-in-law. Judy was eagerly looking forward to working with me in this new combination ministry and independent contractor opportunity.

The quality time also spent with KWAK was reminiscent of only a few months earlier when Judy and I had spent a week with the family at a Christian camp in the Colorado mountains. The trip was so exceptional that we talked about it for the next two years as we recalled the singing, worship, kid stuff, horseback riding, fellowship, fun, worshipful meals, scenery out of a travelogue, and quiet time. Thus, we were both still "singing as we go." God is good, all the time.

Judy and I had been blessed throughout our lives together and were now happily contemplating and actively making plans for a God and family-centered retirement life. The January trip to Jacksonville was to be only the beginning of a new time in our lives. The kids also treated us to a surprise visit to see the beautiful new ocean condo they had bought near St. Augustine, joyfully advising us that we would have access to it as often as we wanted. Life was perfect and I assumed it would continue. But God offers such a guarantee to no man. If I had been asked at that time if I had been pruned enough through life to produce fruit for the Kingdom to the extent God desired of me, I would have unequivocally answered in the affirmative, thereby displaying both arrogance and ignorance.

THE NEWS

Judy's entries on her calendar/diary for two days in the latter part of January 2004 read: "January 23: Doctor's appointment. Couldn't stop coughing night before. Up until 2:00 A.M. Did some tests. Put me on antibiotic Levaquin. Pray it works. January 29: Still coughing. Doctor unsure of test results. Referred me to pulmonologist."

The day before Valentine's Day I took Judy to the appointment set up by her general practitioner. Why had her cough of well over a year never gone away? The cough itself was quite often more nuisance than substance and Judy (as well as I) thought it was probably due to an allergy of some sort. It had required her to sleep on her right side exclusively, however, because of the mucous being generated. That was bothersome to both of us. Our son-in-law, himself an oncologist, had recommended during our trip to Jacksonville earlier that month that we see a specialist when we got home. He had suspected something might be amiss.

The visit to the pulmonologist did not go as we had hoped. The concern in the doctor's face and voice was palpable as she came back into the exam room following the chest x-ray. She said the x-ray presented an abnormal right lung. She qualified that statement by saying it could be due to either pneumonia or to something else. When the doc left the room the nurse seemed bent upon telling us that it was very likely pneumonia. We weren't reassured. A few moments later the doc told us to go and enjoy a nice lunch and then later that afternoon check into the hospital for further testing.

I had made reservations for us for Valentine's dinner the following evening at one of our favorite little restaurants, Café Au

Lait. I promptly called to cancel the next day's dinner and move the reservation up to lunch that very day. We were both understandably emotional and apprehensive over the pulmonologist's vague findings. Over lunch I gave Judy the matching cherry-finish plaque she *didn't* receive at my retirement party. I had it made up to match mine, except for the copy, which read: "Presented to Judy, my wife of 45 years. In love and appreciation for all these years of support and dedication to our marriage, our family, and to our work. We both know full well that we owe everything to God, our provider. In Jesus' name, Terry."

We exchanged cards and I also gave her a small heart-shaped box of chocolates, of which I ended up eating all but five pieces. Her card to me read: "I never dreamed I could feel this close to anyone . . . or love anyone so completely, but you have inspired that love." I then, lovingly and— at times—tearfully, read her a custom-made list headed with, "The Top 20 Things I Most Appreciate About You." The meal was a somber time. A new friend from my Stephen Ministry training was sitting at the next table, so I asked her if she would take a picture of us with the camera I had brought with me. She was happy to oblige. What is Stephen Ministry? It's a ministry of church people who receive nearly 50 hours of training in listening to people who need someone for that purpose and who are willing to commit a minimum of two years to doing so.

We went from there to the North Fulton Regional Hospital (NFRH) in Roswell and checked Judy in that Friday. A few preliminary tests were done on Saturday and then on Sunday a Christian pulmonologist partner of the initial examining doc performed a nasty endoscopy procedure (which I understand has since become much more routine and simpler for the patient). I say "nasty" because it involved running a line with a camera down her throat to photograph her lungs.

Judy was hypersensitive to drugs, so they gave her a less than normal dosage of anesthesia. She was still talking to them as the doc was ready to go forward, however, so they gave her another dose. After a while I overheard the surgical team from my seat in the next room say, "Administer the antidote. She isn't coming around." A few more-than-anxious minutes later I heard the same voice say,

"She's pinking up." Judy heard those same words and within only a few more minutes joked about the experience, commenting about how happy she was that her blue hue had turned pink.

Since that was Sunday, we wouldn't get the results for another day or so. The next morning she underwent another of the many cathode ray tube procedures she was to face in the coming months. She was very apprehensive about these tests because she was not allowed to move or cough. At that first one she allayed her emotions by telling all of the technicians in the room of her concern. She then witnessed to them, saying all she had to do to get through the procedure was ask Jesus to take her hand and let her hold onto the edge of His cloak, just as "the woman in the gospels had done."

About Judy's favorite miraculous Bible story, here is how it reads: " As Jesus passed in a crowd pressing around Him a woman was there who had been subject to bleeding for twelve years, but no one could heal her. She came up behind Him and touched the edge of His cloak, and immediately her bleeding stopped. Jesus asked 'Who touched me?' Peter and the others accompanying him said they had no idea because of the size of the crowd, but Jesus said, 'Someone touched me; I know that power has gone out from me.' Then the woman, seeing that she could not go unnoticed, came trembling and fell at His feet. In the presence of all the people, she told why she had touched Him and how she had been instantly healed. Then He said to her, 'Daughter, your faith has healed you. Go in peace'" (Luke 8:43-48).

This tactic of faith would serve Judy well on many upcoming occasions. She felt that on her own she could not possibly manage to keep from coughing for as long as thirty minutes during each of the many CAT scans and MRIs to come during her chemotherapy treatment and testing. Her trust in the Lord for that help never once failed her.

At around the dinner hour on Monday following the definitive Sunday testing I went down to the hospital cafeteria for a short break. We hadn't yet gotten results of the tests. When I returned, Judy was sitting on the edge of her bed. The only other person in the room was her roommate, a sympathetic but non-believing Jewish lady who had a myriad of problems of her own and with whom I had prayed the day before. Judy had a noticeably subdued countenance and said softly, "The physician's assistant (the third partner in the pulmonologist's office) called (called, mind you, not visited) to say the diagnosis was non-smoker's broncho-alveolar lung cancer." Then she added the heart-breaking qualifier, "It's inoperable."

I was stunned. My first reaction–I guess because I didn't want to accept the news—was sort of a re-direct. I said, "He told you that over the phone?" Judy responded simply, saying, "Yes." Then we fell sobbing into each other's arms as she added, "I wanted to be so brave." I only remember two other times in the nineteen months to follow when she would say, "I tried to be so strong."

During that one-week diagnostic stay in the hospital she was a model patient with doctors, nurses, fellow patients, technicians and cleaning personnel. She witnessed to each of them, expressing optimism, cheerfulness, and absolute trust in Christ Jesus, her Lord and Savior. I once asked her about her nature in that regard and she said, "It's important to be kind. Every one you meet is fighting a hard battle." The Lord doesn't ask so much *how* we are doing, but *what* we are doing for others.

By the time I took her home I knew in my heart that in the weakness of her body Judy would find strength in Christ to carry her mind and soul through the ordeal. I did two things that day in response to where she and I were in our new journey. First—and in private–I cried and wailed to God as I prayed for both of us. Then I asked God to help me, to give me strength and comfort. He instantly dried up my tears, although they would return again and again.

Every time I would follow Judy's lead in asking the Lord for help He would always do so. From that day forward I have prayed that I might have her degree of faith, conviction and strength in facing life's trials. I tried to trust completely in God, including the upcoming trials of Judy's cancer, even though I had every reason to think they would ultimately lead to her untimely death. After all, if she had such faith in the face of her own trials, why shouldn't I?

During the nineteen-plus months between Judy's diagnosis the week of February 13, 2004 and the week following her September 23, 2005 passing I found great therapy in journaling our odyssey through some 325 single-spaced pages. In addition to the journaling,

I sent monthly e-mail updates to family and friends concerning Judy's condition. Shortly after that start I also began including relevant gospel-based messages along with the updates. Over time my audience grew from only a dozen or so family names to today's modest ministry newsletter of more than 500 e-mailed recipients.

This book is not intended to be a personal journal, but for purposes of this writing effort, i.e., the lessons of God's pruning for a more productive life, and for those people who have been spared, left behind, or still suffering, I will now draw upon selected entries from that journal and the accompanying messages. I feel the Lord has especially blessed me through Judy's truly remarkable witness in placing her trust so completely with Him.

LIFE RESUMES

In late February, only a week or so after Judy's diagnosis, we went to church service and sat in one of the two large "crying/coughing" rooms. Judy's cough was unremitting. Afterwards, both of our sons and their wives came to our house with food and good spirits. Our oldest son's wife asked Judy what stage she was in. We hadn't known to ask the doctor such a question and no one had volunteered such information. Thus, we didn't yet know Judy was already in stage four (end stage). I believe that early diagnosis of a disease is of little value unless it results in a better prognosis. Thus, we never had regrets about not having an earlier diagnosis of her slow-growing and broadly diffused lung cancer. What you do know can hurt you. We could have spent many more months, even years, with much less quality of life trying to unsuccessfully treat her cancer.

That evening Judy and I spent an hour and a half going over details of how she kept our personal and business books. That was her idea and I barely managed to get through it. The next day I spoke by phone with my friend and boss, David, in my newly-acquired support role with Shalom Network. He called from the Ukraine and asked me to re-read the gospels and the book of Acts for Jesus' miracles, and then pray like this: "Lord, I want my own miracle. How shall I pray for it?" He also said he would do a 24-hour fast for Judy the following week. In doing so he thus inspired me to do my own first-ever 24-hour fast with prayer the next day.

That very next day Judy and I had a short Bible study together about three specific miracles in Scripture which I read to her from Matthew, Mark, and Luke. We prayed for miraculous healing. She especially asked that I read the passage having to do with Jesus healing a man's withered hand, but always she most related to the healing miracle of the touching of Jesus' hem by the hemorrhaging woman.

How much has God done for us that we can begin to understand his love for us and thereby our need to love Him and our neighbor, as His two greatest commandments to us? This is something Judy and I talked about, that out of love for the Father, the eternal Son—or as one pastor puts it, "the Son of His love,"—volunteered to take upon Himself a human nature. His love would involve physical suffering and dying.

I asked myself about the particulars of that act. God cannot suffer bodily because He is a spirit; so God would have to take upon Himself a nature that could suffer. And, as Don Kistler expresses this concept, the eternal God could neither die, nor could he cease to be, even for one moment. Therefore, the Son would have to become a man so that He could die. As the Son in human form, He would then do all that was necessary to purchase those whom God determined to love from before He laid the foundations of the world.

Thus, it is through our faith that we get "born again," and as a result we believe. The lessons I was beginning to learn from understanding Judy's absolute trust were a part of my pruning, but I had difficulty when my thoughts turned to questioning God over possibly punishing Judy for my own inadequacies. It would take a long time for me to get over that hurdle. In time I would come to understand that her faith had ultimately resulted in her healing in God's presence.

When our youngest son came to visit his mother in the early weeks and they had a therapeutic cry, Judy comforted him. She understood the apt Scripture lesson from Jeremiah 29:11-12: 'For I know the plans I have for you,' declares the Lord. 'plans to prosper you and not to harm you, plans to give you hope and a future.' But what "hope" I still wondered, if the patient dies?

Later, I read the following from the book of Hebrews: "The Father, like He did with Christ, often uses suffering to set us apart for His work even though we cannot always see how He is doing this while the suffering is taking place." Prophetically, Judy suggested to me that I look back later in life to see how God used her suffering to further the Kingdom. Even now I cannot help but weep as I think about her suggestion. I now dwell on the ministries both Helga and I are involved in, singly and as a married couple, and think of how broad Judy's faith was in so many respects.

WINDS OF CHANGE

As I began the regular Judy-update and ministry newsletters, which in time would become–first, through Judy's inspiration and then later through Helga's encouragement, as well as through thankfulness for my own "new days"—the *New Day Newsletter*, I offered this prayer in print shortly after her diagnosis. Forgive its extensiveness.

"Dear Lord, you know Judy, your child and my wife of 45 years, and that she was diagnosed with inoperable stage four lung cancer several weeks ago. You also know that she seeks to comfort rather than be comforted, just one of the many gifts you have given her. This morning we took time to joyfully look inside two special "rooms" of life. Of course you were there to see the joy which greeted us in that first room, the one of Countless Personal Blessings. Here I have listed only a few of those blessings which the Holy Spirit has left us with such sweet memories:

* Judy's and my love for each other since the age of 18, truly a gift from you, Father.
* Our three children, each of whom has blessed us through their childhood, their completed education, their trustworthiness, their self-discipline, their loving marriages, and their love for us.
* Our three in-law children whom we love as our own.
* Our two precious grandchildren, with perhaps (assuredly) more to come.

- Our family brothers and sisters who have not only shared much of their lives with us but have also taken their turn in caring for aging parents, ill spouses and the challenges of child-rearing.
- Judy's unceasing prayer life since you first consoled her in early childhood.

- My return to you after a 40-year hiatus, which was entirely through Your prevenient grace.
- The body of Christ as exemplified by the support and uplifting from both our church and others.
- Terry's good health so that he might be able to stand when Judy must rest.
- Life itself, and indeed our life in Christ, thereby assuring us that through our faith alone in His resurrection we, too, will defeat death and gain eternal life in Your presence.
- Our wonderful life in this country of milk and honey, which we did not choose but were given.
- The many memorable adventures and times shared with each other, our family and best friends.
- The work and the industry that not only provided us (through you, Lord) our bread for 40 years.

"Most importantly, Lord, thank you for the realization that the ability to be joyful always, to pray continually, and to give thanks in all circumstances comes only from a strong belief in the promises of Scripture that these things are Your will and by the Holy Spirit are blown through our lives in the name of Jesus Christ.

"And then, Lord, after Judy and I breathed deeply of your grace for our Countless Personal Blessings and left that special place, we risked opening the door to the second of the two rooms. This was the room in which the world's crosses are stored. At my urging (not of Judy's desire) and with only my personal complaint of the cross we were carrying, You yet invited our entry into the Room of Inventoried Crosses. Once inside–knowing of my prayer for a lighter cross—you not only welcomed us, you invited me to deposit our cross and to take up another of my choosing. You recall that I excitedly glanced at Judy, but she—being a prayer intercessor and having seen the weight of crosses so many others bear–simply shook her head and smiled at me through her tears of understanding.

"As you know, there are tens of thousands of crosses scattered about that huge room, including many quite large ones, and one monstrous execution stake that only One could possibly carry. I was looking for a small cross as I searched relentlessly through the room. Finally I found what I was looking for. You saw me dash to pick it up and then quickly grab Judy by the arm before thankfully exiting. Outside the door I held her to me and prayed to You, 'Thank you, Lord. This cross we can bear.'

"You replied, 'I know, Son. It's the one with which you entered.'

"Thank you for the humbling lesson, Lord. I will try to do better. While I now understand that deep faith *may* make a difference in how Judy's system responds to her cancer, I more fully realize that deep faith *absolutely* makes a difference through everlasting life. It is in His name that we live and pray. Amen."

TRIBULATION

I'm wary of the cliche that goes, "Cheer up. Things could be worse." One day before Judy's first scheduled chemo treatment I received a call from a nurse at my mother's assisted living facility. The message was that my mother, 87 years old at the time, had fallen and fractured her hip and was in the hospital. In reacting to strong medication she was convinced of a hospital conspiracy, certain that various people there wanted to kill her. She was reasonably certain gentle Judy was not a part of it but I received no such specific clearance.

That same evening Judy and I sat on the couch and held hands while watching our favorite CD, *Singin' In The Rain*. After a quiet meal at which we sat side-by-side at the table, I wondered if we would ever watch that CD together again. We agreed that we would no longer take telephone calls if we were having a meal.

Later that evening our daughter, Wendi, and and son-in-law, Kevin, called and asked us to think about taking a trip with them, perhaps to Alaska. Judy said the only trip she *might* consider would be to Jacksonville in order to see KWAK (Kevin, Wendi, Abigail and Karsten). She would never again leave the greater Atlanta area.

I had been praying over my lack of faith that Judy would be healed. The Father answered me just before I retired for the night. Rushing downstairs for the copy of Strong's Concordance given to me years earlier by my son-in-law, I shortly found myself reading Matthew 14:30-31., one of the verse references for "trust." Jesus had rebuked Peter for not trusting Him after he had begun walking towards Him on the water. Peter began to sink, however, when the wind came up and he lost his focus on Christ. I began to pray a bit differently, substituting "trust" in Him for my desires.

Judy's cough was getting much worse. To me, it sounded ominous. God gave me yet another answer concerning our grief and how He fully understands. Judy and I had each other to comfort us personally, but God could not reach down and comfort His Son at the time of greatest need because Jesus the man was still covered by the sins of man, about to pay the sacrificial price for us. Had the Father comforted the Son at that particular time, the Father's justified wrath could not have been expiated. That would have been tempered justice rather than righteous justice. Knowing this I suddenly realized that the Father knew exactly where we were. In effect, He was saying, "Don't you think I know about your grief?"

2 Corinthians 4:8 speaks to this very thing: "We are hard pressed on every side, but not crushed; perplexed, but not in despair."

STRENGTH THROUGH HIM

As I began attending church alone most Sundays, many people told me they were praying for Judy. One night I went to the hospital to check on Mom and found that things were out of control for her, mentally, emotionally and physically. I called Judy from the hospital to check on her and her voice was so weak that I was engulfed in sadness for her and pity for myself. I walked around the parking lot in darkness, sobbing and crying out to God. I prayed for His help.

In another hour or so I arrived home expecting Judy to be in even worse condition than when I had left. Although she couldn't do more than whisper she was, incredibly, working on our taxes! Sensing that I was vulnerable from the day she comforted me. She comforted *me*!

Over the next week or so Judy showed me how to do a wash. Yeah. I know. Don't say it. Martin worked extra hours so he could come over one afternoon to videotape a household inventory. Judy put on her new blue denim hat that looked so cute on her. Actually, she looked more beautiful than cute. I asked her if she wanted to go out for dinner that evening and she enthusiastically accepted, requesting we visit a special cheeseburger, fries and malted milk shake joint. That foray had been our first meal outing since before going to the hospital for her diagnosis.

I gassed up her car several days later, not knowing when she might drive again. She never did. She hadn't driven her little white Toyota station wagon since two days before her diagnosis. Our prayer life became very positive during that same time frame. Both of us had been assigned a Stephen Minister, although Judy had been surprisingly reluctant in that regard. When I asked her about that she said she did not want to take a Stephen Minister away from ministering to someone who *really* needed the help. I asked her if she was afraid of what was happening. She said she didn't cry for herself, only for others whenever she got a card, phone call or e-mail of support for her.

The Lord gives and the Lord takes away. Just as with the apostle Paul we were trying to be content with what the Lord had taken away as well as with what He had provided. Question: What *is* the fruit that comes with pruning? Abraham did not need to be afraid of anything for the Lord God declared to him–as He has to us—that He Himself is our reward, that His grace is enough. He is our Shield, our Guardian, our Protector, and what is more, our exceedingly great Reward. And Judy— far more than me at the time—understood that God's refining fires were for exactly that. We are told that pruning is not intended as punishment, but for greater productivity. I still wasn't certain of my clearance in that regard.

PLANS A, B, & C

We didn't know God's plan for Judy at the time but we had exhausted man's Plan A–the first chemo treatment with dual drugs–between the mid-February diagnosis and the first of June 2004. Her primary oncologist advised us at that time that the latest chest x-ray showed she had actually lost ground rather than improving. Next, came Man's Plan B, an oral treatment which I labeled "the pill that couldn't be swallowed," and not for its size. Since the IRESSA pill did not involve intravenous injection Medicare mindlessly decided to label the treatment as "not valid for coverage." The bottom line was that the cost to us would run $1,800 a month (for 30 $60 pills), an expense we were not prepared to handle. It was at that time that our son-in-law stepped forward and without a second thought said that if we could get no help from the patient assistance programs some pharmaceutical firms offer (which we discovered we could not), that he and our daughter would cover us.

Our Atlanta oncologist had been enthusiastic over the drug's possibilities, citing some past–although scant—successes. After six weeks of being on that plan, however, the doc called us in to hear him say words my ears could hear, but my emotions could not handle. As I held Judy's hand he said, "The IRESSA drug is not working. You really have only two choices at this point. The first is another IV drug, although it comes with some of the usual, but not as nasty, side effects as her first-line treatment. We can try that for at least two cycles (six weeks)." He went on to qualify the option, saying, "It won't cure you, but it might buy you some time."

"And what's the second choice?" I asked. "Pain management," he said, giving us what must be the news oncologists most dislike sharing with a patient who is not progressing through treatment. My heart leapt to my throat and tried to throttle me. Before I could even glance at Judy I mumbled, "Hospice. That's a death sentence."

"It's actually called hospice-at-home," he responded as gently as he could, adding, "Do you want to try the drug?" My heart broke again as I embraced her. No one said anything for several moments. Then Judy broke the silence with more hope and courage than I could imagine, saying, "Well, if we can't make it together, one of us will carry on."

She opted to try the last-ditch drug. When we went to the hospital cafeteria for lunch a short time later we bowed our heads in prayer. As her "rock" I was still so emotionally overcome with the doctor's pronouncement that I was not able to utter a single word beyond, "Our heavenly Father . . ." As a former geologist I know there are many kinds of rocks and minerals. At that moment I was a piece of soapstone–a rock so soft a fingernail can scratch it. Judy's will at that moment, however, could have scratched a diamond. After gently comforting me with, "It'll be all right," she told the Lord exactly what she thought of Him. She praised Him for His mercy in showing us yet another "plan" we could try.

What an incredible privilege it is to be a caregiver to one's wife. It was at that moment that I realized we loved each other even more than we had when we first began dating in high school 47 years earlier. And just as importantly we realized that God was not only in control but that He reveals Himself to us in sorrow and tragedy as much as in the fullness and happiness of life.

DOUBLING UP

Valorie, the Stephen Ministry leader at Mt. Pisgah as well as having a host of other church responsibilities, called Judy, wanting to make her first caring visit as a representative of this incredible listening and caring ministry. Their slogan is so simple: "God cures, we care." Within a few more hours I also received a call. That one from another Stephen Minister. He had been assigned to care for me during our crisis. Ironically, I had begun my own training as a Stephen Minister only two months earlier. I had another two and a half months of training yet to come.

It was March 23, Judy's and my 45th wedding anniversary. Her temperature had been at the 100 degree mark for two days and she was taking 400 mg of Tylenol every two hours but with little improvement. In the middle of all of this my mother, who had been falling from the early stages of dementia into a much more severe state, called and said she felt she was "going crazy." I consoled her as best I could and asked if she was ready to go down for dinner at her assisted living facility. She said, "the two little boys aren't here yet." I asked her what she meant and she said, "You know, Terry and Mike." Judy overheard the conversation and we wept silently, embracing one another. Mom had put herself back in time, to pre-1943 before my youngest brother, Dave, had been born.

The very next day, however, was a wonderful one for us. Judy had the most beautiful and radiant smile all day. She kept giving me her cute little "thumbs up" second-signature trademark. That was usually followed by her "V" for Victory-in-Jesus' split two-fingered sign. She left an article for me at the table which concerned the "unspeakable gift" from God. That gift, of course, is His Son, who provides eternal salvation for all who believe on Him.

I particularly recall the day following that one, thinking that it was one of the most enjoyable days of my entire life. We did a wash together as Judy gently explained the routine to me once again. We found blessings in everything we did together. She read me a different translation of her favorite Scripture verses, 1 Thessalonians 5:16-18: "Rejoice evermore. In everything give thanks: for this is the will of God in Christ Jesus concerning you." She never became self-absorbed, she did not despair, and she certainly did not blame God for her circumstances. As strange as it seemed to me at the time, she considered her illness as preparation for an even more productive life in Christ! She actually considered herself still being refined by God's fires, such that she could become yet more Christ-like between then and when He would call her home.

REPEATING OUR VOWS

On Sunday, March 28, our youngest son and his wife, Betty, arrived after having picked up our daughter and granddaughter at the airport. Shortly after that our eldest son and his wife, Wheng, also arrived. Wendi ushered a squeaky-voiced—but otherwise full-of-life—Judy into the living room, a pretty blue turban hiding her lost hair. Martin asked me to go upstairs with him. He immediately closed the door and handed me an envelope. Inside was a beautifully printed invitation requesting my presence at the remarriage of his mother and me. I broke down in tears.

But there was more to come. Wendi insisted I put on a white shirt and jacket to go with the Fred Astaire-like top hat, the button-holed Boutonniere, and the "groom" pin they had brought me. Wendi had done essentially the same thing with Judy and she reacted just as I had. The ceremony was to take place right there and then. In a reversal of ceremony and at their cue, I (not Judy) slowly walked down the stairs. Our living room had been decorated and our favorite Big Band music was playing. There on the couch sat my beautiful bride, wearing a flowered veil. I took my seat beside her. Then Jason sat beside me as he prepared to give his mother away.

Within a minute or two, Mike, our good friend and our church's minister of caring surprised us as he walked—beaming—into the room. In a very emotional ceremony he had us repeat our wedding vows of 45 years earlier. Before that, however, he reiterated for us the Bible's very clear definition of love. He read from 1 Corinthians 13:4-5: "Love is patient, love is kind. It does not envy, it does not boast, it is not proud. It is not rude, it is not self-seeking, it is not easily angered, it keeps no record of wrongs. It always protects, always trusts, always hopes, always perseveres."

In response I eagerly asked if I could kiss the bride. Request granted. The least-used room in the house had yet again served its very special purpose, adding to such past events as my asking challenging engagement questions of our daughter's soon-to-be-successful suitor, and counter- evangelizing Jehovah's Witnesses and Mormon house calls.

PRAISE AND PRAYER

After finishing the second night of the worst two days of Judy's ordeal since the onset of her illness, during which she coughed so continuously from midnight to one A.M., we simply sat on the bed and held hands. As we professed our love for one another and for almighty God we softly wept. The next day we received a phone call from the Philippines, from Wheng's mother. She had Wheng's five-year old cousin on the phone and he told Judy that he loved her and then chattered joyously into her ear before concluding the conversation by calling her "grandma." Little Mark Bryan suffered from leukemia but one would never know it from his attitude. Judy was elated at the call. She would never get to meet the little Philippino boy she so wanted to love.

On Good Friday, Judy and I spoke of the celebration James Durham writes about in his book, *The Blessed Death of Those Who Die in the Lord*. The point of the title has to do with the lamentable fact of "how few there are"—even among the great multitudes of professing Christians—"of pretenders to the hope which attends them who die in the Lord that truly understand the purpose of life." What he is saying is that so few make it the great business of their life to live through all the days of their appointed time coveting the Lord and thanking Him in prayer. Thanking Him for what? That He would so graciously and effectually be teaching them, as Moses put it, "to number their days that they may apply their hearts to wisdom."

On that 2004 Easter Sunday, as I was preparing to go to church without her, Judy did not ask me to pray for her. What she did ask was to, "Praise Him for me." She had been watching a Judy Garland

Christmas movie the night before and commented that it had gotten her to thinking that she might not have a Christmas that year. Then, she added the reason for her praise request: "I realized that this sort of thinking is not of God, for He provides for us and we are not to worry about tomorrow."

Her simple and selfless prayer request reminds me of something another author has written on the subject. Peter Kreeft's words are these: "I strongly suspect that if we saw all the difference even the tiniest of our prayers make, and all the people those little prayers were destined to affect, and all the consequences of our prayers down through the centuries, we would be so paralyzed with awe at the power of prayer that we would be unable to get up off our knees for the rest of our lives."

HOSPITALIZED

A few nights later, as we sat on the couch watching a wonderful movie together, Judy developed a coughing bout that was so severe I rubbed her back through it all. At about two A.M. she woke me saying she felt a sharp "punch" on one side of her lungs. It subsided, then recurred, then again subsided. At four A.M. she got up to go to the bathroom and felt the same "punch" again, but this time it was on the other side of her lungs. When she was later asked about the pain, she said on a scale of one-to-ten it was a nine. I had never known her to describe her pain as anything beyond a six or seven. As she was returning from the bathroom she fell against the folding closet doors, ricocheted off of them and onto the bed, all but passing out. I immediately got her dressed and drove her to the emergency room at Piedmont Hospital in midtown Atlanta. Within an hour or so she was diagnosed with pneumonia.

One day the next week, as she continued her recovery from the pneumonia, she asked me if we could "take a walk in the park." What she meant was a walk around the nurse's station. As we did, she commented on the many names I had for her, one of them (Fluffy) being something she had seen years ago in a needlepoint catalog depicting two little sheep kids or babies. The caption had read, "Ewes not fat. Ewes fluffy." She had a good laugh from recalling the memory. What a wonderful medicine, laughter.

When I came home from the hospital that early evening, our lawn guy and his wife were there, taking care of our lawn. Through the patio door he motioned for me to come outside. Once there he hugged me with tears in his eyes as he asked about Judy. As he did so he shared with me that he worked six days a week from 2:00 A.M. until 8:00 P.M., and that if he had all the money he needed he would only tend to six yards and that ours (although the smallest of them all) would be one of them.

I took Judy a get well card that got a big laugh from her while she was still in the hospital. I had taped a short piece of a light cord, including the plug, to the inside of her card. The card read "No one is going to pull the plug on you, sweetheart." Later that day, when her oncologist visited during his hospital rounds, he brought up the subject of Judy's "quality of life." She said, "Hey, I have a wonderful quality of life." Then she handed her card to him and added, "Look at my warranty." The doc was still laughing when he left the room.

WHAT CHEER?

If you had lived in a very small mid-1800s pioneer community and felt you were much blessed in life as you were about to participate in naming your very small community, what name might you suggest for that purpose? Judy and I both grew up in a small central Iowa town about fifty miles from such a village, one whose population still does not warrant a listing in most road atlases. The name of the village is What Cheer.

As high school students in the mid-1950s we all made fun of the village's name, as in "Where is he (or she) from? What Cheer?" The "clever" remark was always followed by snickers from the sophisticated. After all, our town of Newton was well over the 15,000 population mark.

But what do you suppose possessed the town fathers of What Cheer to choose such a name? I don't know the actual history behind that decision, but I can speculate that in the mid-1800s it might well have been due to a typical rural midwestern community's faith in Jesus Christ as their Lord and Savior.

What cheer the folks in that area must have taken in the Lord! I can imagine a scenario 150 or so years ago when the families living there might have decided on a town naming day. They may have gathered together at a special time–perhaps at a Summer's picnic on a Sunday afternoon. They would have been working hard all merely to survive and continue making a small way for themselves. They would then have carved out time to honor and thank the Father on the Lord's Day.

What cheer they must have had in Him that Summer afternoon, Bibles in hand. Perhaps someone read from the book of John concerning Jesus' summation to His disciples in His last moments with them. Perhaps they were the words from chapter 16, verse 33 (KJV, the Bible translation surely most common at the time): "These things I have spoken unto you, that in me ye might have peace. In the world ye shall have tribulation: but be of good cheer; I have overcome the world." Someone might have responded to the reading with, "Say, that gives me an idea for a name: 'What Cheer!'"

What is my point? Whenever someone would ask Judy how she was doing, she would invariably answer, "I'm doing great!" Why was that? Was it because she was Pollyannaish about life? Not at all. Some might say she was an eternal optimist. Well, maybe so, but more to the point she was a woman of good cheer. And for good reason. In the above Scripture Jesus was telling His disciples to take courage, to be of good cheer in spite of the inevitable struggles they would face. He was telling them they would not be alone, that He would never leave them. Neither does He abandon you nor me to our troubles, for the Holy Spirit is always with us. If we remember that the ultimate victory has already been won, we can claim the peace of Christ in the most troublesome times.

Let me share with you another example. One day, minutes after one of Judy's regular visits to the oncologist during which we received particularly bad news, we unexpectedly met a friend at a restaurant next to the hospital. We hadn't seen or talked to him in some time and all he knew was that Judy was undergoing chemotherapy. We were just finishing our lunch and he asked how Judy was doing. In response to his question, Judy smiled beautifully and said, "I'm doing great!" She didn't want to discomfort our friend, whom she knew had his own problems.

What cheer! But there is even greater meaning here than the above. Judy trusted in the Lord for whatever He had in store for her, even if she didn't understand everything. After the fact, she knew the Lord obviously did not plan for chemotherapy to cure her. Therefore, she understood the Lord had other plans for her and that whatever those plans were she would continue to trust Him, praise Him, and remain thankful for His grace and the countless mercies already extended to her. She had the peace that passes understanding and thus could remain of good cheer, whatever the circumstances.

HOPE SPRINGS FROM THE HEART

Still in the hospital and voiceless, Judy sat in a chair and wrote on a pad for me to read, "Maybe God is healing the cancer this way." She was referring to the drainage of more than 600 ccs of liquid from the bag in her chest cavity outside her lungs.

The next day I answered an e-mail from Sandy in the Ukraine. She had asked what God was saying to us. After pondering that question for several days my best e-mail answer was that God might simply be telling us that His grace is sufficient. Both Judy and I were not only okay with that, but feeling blessed about it.

At church service our pastor spoke about how to pray, and that blockages to effective prayer can be caused by our not having forgiven certain people in our lives. I immediately thought of the physician's assistant who so insensitively told Judy of her diagnosis over the phone instead of coming to her room. He had compounded that insensitivity the very next day when Judy asked him how serious things were. His reply had been matter-of-fact and without apparent concern as he said simply, "Get your affairs in order." Until that moment in church I had not come close to forgiving him, but the sermon convicted me and I saw to that forgiveness. Judy had long before forgiven him.

She would have to make a much more difficult decision than that one, however, before she was able to come home from the hospital. That decision had to do with letting go of her beloved little white toy poodle, Muffy. We simply could no longer care for her, what with all the hospital and doctor trips. Muffy not only suffered from serious separation anxiety but we were also advised that the germs a dog can carry could easily impact an immune-deficient cancer patient.

A young female technician at the veterinarian's office which had been serving our animal needs for 25 years had told us more than once that she would love to have Muffy if we ever wanted to give her up. I was elected to take care of this as Judy was too heart-broken over the decision to accompany me once she got home. Muffy was unquestionably Judy's doggie, yet I was very emotional at the actual hand-over. I loved the little doggie also, but I believe my emotion that day had much more to do with the broader implications of the moment. The good news is that ever since that day Muffy has thrived under Denise's care. She even calls and sometimes writes me with updates, including pictures.

The time was early May and our daughter and granddaughter arrived from Jacksonville, going directly to the hospital. What a blessing for us at that time in our lives that Wendi was home-schooling Abigail. She could bring her along and still provide her with lessons. Once home, Judy presented me for my birthday the most beautiful solid gold cross on a chain. It was made in a three-nail design, with a Star of David on one side and the initial "J" on the other. That symbolized both Jesus and Judy. On the bottom of the cross (on the head of one of the nails) was engraved our wedding date. My eyes filled with tears as I lovingly accepted it and put it on. I have continued to proudly wear it to this day, never inside my shirt, but always outside. As much as any personal possession I have, this necklace expresses the hope I have in Christ for everlasting life.

LESSONS COME FASTER

Before Judy became too ill to have much of anything for a morning meal she would breakfast on a bowl of Cheerios and a plate of four dehydrated prunes, which I would first stew for her. She would alert me to her interest in that regard by cheerfully calling to me on the intercom with, "Teh-wee, I'm awake." I would then bound upstairs, eager to greet the new day with her.

One day she said she couldn't manage walking between the three different appointments I had scheduled for her in midtown Atlanta. The first was with her oncologist for a shot of Procrit to build up her depleted red blood cells; the second was with the pulmonologist for a check on her lungs; and the third was with the infectious disease doc to monitor the bacterial infection in her pleural sac. She said she would need extra strength for the task. We solved the problem by borrowing my mother's wheelchair. The Lord always provides.

It was mid-May and I was finishing up my Stephen Ministry training along with the other twenty trainees of the nearly five-month program. Our commissioning would be on the Sunday following, but we would conclude the actual training the day before with foot washing. The point about that ceremony from group leader Valorie was very clear. "If you aren't ready to have your feet washed, you aren't ready to wash your care receiver's feet."

Coincidentally, the commissioning came on my 66th birthday. Valorie had gotten a crying room assigned to my family so that Judy's unremitting cough would not keep her away. The make-up for that room would include Jude in a wheelchair, along with RAWBi-the-oxygen tank, plus my mother, and son Martin. The head usher told me they would actually lock the crying room's door from the outside so as to ensure our privacy.

Approximately 2,000 people were seated for that particular service, which concluded not only with our commissioning but with our same group serving communion to the congregation. What a blessing to have each person coming forward look us squarely in the eyes as we offered them first the bread, accompanied by the words, "The body of Christ broken for you." Similarly, the juice was offered with the words, "The blood of Christ shed for you." At my station one young boy hesitatingly took the bread and instead of simply dipping it into the juice he dropped it into the goblet. The Holy Spirit surely guided me as I gave him another piece while his father fished out the miscued piece, avoiding embarrassment for the youth. Just as quickly, an usher replaced my juice goblet for those next in line.

The essence of senior pastor Hunt's message that day was that as wonderful as one's living witness is for others to see, no one has ever been converted merely from that observation. Words are needed. The question that immediately came to my mind was, "What would I say if someone were to ask me about Jesus?" I have since come to the conclusion that when anyone asks me about Him, my best initial witness is to tell them how I came to believe and how much Christ has meant to me.

Two days later—on Judy's own 66th birthday—we humbly read from the book of Job one of the most meaningful verses in the Bible for those struggling with life's most difficult lessons: "Shall we accept good from God, and not trouble?" The point here is that if we thank God for His blessings in our lives–which means we acknowledge that He knows what is best for us–how can we not accept that He also knows our trials will (somehow, ultimately) be for our good?

Over and over, Judy demonstrated her trust in God by being as obedient to Him as she could. By that I mean she was increasingly empowered to think more and more in a way that she would not ordinarily do. As she grew in Christ through her affliction she allowed the "new woman" in her to flower. She lived through her relationship with Christ. And as she grew ever more faithful and trusting she pushed out more and more of herself, allowing more and more of Christ to be apparent in her.

During those nineteen months of her illness I could readily see her continuing growth in Christ. And as I uncomfortably look back at the time I recognize that I was limping in my own walk relative to Judy's. What prompts me to say that? Not too many months following my own conversion–after 50+ years of Judy's walking with the Lord–I zealously asked her if she had actually confessed her faith by mouth. At that moment I was as guilty as the Pharisees in thinking they were bound by the Law.

When I was confirmed at about age 12–as I said earlier–I did not have a relationship with the Lord. In other words, my "acceptance" of Christ as my Lord and Savior was not heartfelt. Therefore, when–at age 58–I *did* genuinely accept Him, the "old man" (old Creation) died and I was born again as a new Creation. It was then that I asked the Holy Spirit to help me begin feeding the new man and starving the old man. In other words, I am not the man I used to be.

WITNESSING OF A DIFFERENT SORT

Judy and I received an e-mail from a Hebrew Christian friend of mine inviting us to attend with him a talk at the largest orthodox Jewish synagogue in Atlanta, where the senior rabbi had announced he would address Jesus as the Jewish Messiah. Wow! Judy could not manage going, but I joined him for the talk. I was disappointed to listen to perhaps the least inspired speaker I had heard in the previous twenty years. He first admitted to neither having read nor truly known anything of Christian theology and added that he would not respond to questions from the audience. Great start, huh?

The rabbi first made some outrageous statements. One was that the roots of the Messiah are not a solution to the problems of the world, but that the problems of the world are with the roots of the Messiah. In spite of the rabbi's warning not to ask him any questions, my friend raised his hand and asked why it was so difficult to believe that God, the Creator of the universe, could put Himself on earth in the flesh. The speaker's answer was that there is no purpose in knowing God, but in simply serving Him. He then added that the world is not beyond redemption, but rather is outside redemption. Say what?

The lesson of the extent to which people of no faith in God the Father's declared Way was further underscored by another statement by the speaker that "nothing is inherently evil in the world and since it is still suffering and war is ever present, Jesus can't be the Messiah." He wasn't long into that line of talk before he also commented that Jesus could not be the Messiah because he hadn't fulfilled all of the Hebrew Scriptures' prophecies. Well, the fact is that He did fulfill every single Messianic prophecy pertaining to His first coming!

As I sat in the center of the rabbi's frontal line of sight I made eye contact with him at least twice, my three-nail cross necklace with the Star of David superimposed on it easily visible from that distance. I had to write down my comment on the evaluation form at the talk's conclusion, which was that I believe in the Jewish Messiah as prophesied in the Hebrew Scriptures–most particularly in Isaiah 53:5–and as fulfilled in the New Covenant. When I returned home Judy insisted I fill her in on every detail.

MINISTRY WORKING

As I left church the next Sunday I hurried to catch up with a friend striding purposefully in the parking lot, and whom I could see was quite distressed. He gave me an unusually firm hug and I asked him if everything was okay. He assured me it was but his face betrayed him. I asked him again and he said things were definitely *not* going well. As I listened to his story we were both tearful and I suggested that a Stephen Minister would be a good thing for him. Within two days I would become his Stephen Minister. At the same time both Judy and I were being ministered to by other Stephen Ministers! The lesson here is that God cares about us being compassionate *all* the time, not merely when it is convenient.

Later that week, Bob, the close friend mentioned earlier called to check on Judy. I had been witnessing to him for years with little success, but whenever he talked with Judy he would say to me afterwards: "She blows him away with her faith and cheerfulness." I believe God chose to use Judy as His instrument with Bob as often as He did me. When Bob died unexpectedly fewer than two years later and I spoke at his funeral, I credited Judy for leading him to whatever relationship he might have gained with the Lord.

I end this segment with a poor witness on my part as I shamefully share what I had done one day to heap coals on my sin of pride. This is what I wrote in my journal: "At about dinner time on May 24 the accumulated stresses on me claimed my sensitivity as I blamed Judy for our having missed our dinner hour together by her being on the phone for forty minutes. I would later that evening apologize to her for my little tirade. It took until the early morning hours for me to become contrite enough to also ask God's forgiveness."

FAMILIAL LOVE AND SUPPORT

Judy was very excited about the upcoming 2004 Memorial Day week and the prospect of having all eleven members of our immediate family present under the same roof for part of that time. It was Saturday, and after attending my early morning Men of the Way meeting I picked up KWAK at the Atlanta airport. While Wendi and Kevin took Abigail to enjoy a horse camp in nearby Rome for the week, Karsten would stay at Camp Grandpa and Grandma. What a blessing was our then six-year old as he asked 1) why grandma wore a turban, 2) why she had no hair, 3) would it grow back, and 4) why the medicine caused her to lose her hair?

Over dinner that night, with much of the family assembled, little K's father asked him if he would like to say the blessing. To our joyful surprise he did, not only spontaneously thanking Jesus for the food, but asking God to bless everyone in the room, naming each of us, and concluded his beautiful prayer by asking the Lord for healing for his grandmother.

I asked Kevin on the way back from a fitness workout what to expect down the road with respect to Judy's cancer. His gentle but candid words so saddened me that all I could do was weep as I drove. I recall asking myself at the time if that was the *latest* worst day of my life.

Kevin had said that if God did not heal her, or the final IV treatment series was not successful, she would continue to grow weaker and would decrease her activity even more. Following that she would not want to get out of bed. After that, he said her breathing would become even more labored, requiring morphine. He lovingly explained that a further problem would be that increased morphine would likely cause other complications that would result in her systems shutting down, and that would interfere with her sleep. Finally, he explained that she would then sleep until she was with the Lord.

When we got home my daughter handed me the phone and pointed to an e-mail she had just taken from my computer. It said that Judy's 85-year old mother was in a coma and would not likely revive. I immediately dashed upstairs to comfort Judy as she was talking on the phone with her middle sister. Before the day had ended Judy would compose her last letter to her mother, to be read to her by her sisters. Even while in a coma, people are thought to be able to hear and understand talk of things from people very close to them.

Judy and I accompanied Wendi and Abigail to the hair salon for yet another lesson for me. Both of them had their locks shorn to a minimum ten-inch hair length for donation to Locks of Love, an organization which accepts human hair donations from those with unbleached heads, to be used to make human hair wigs for children with cancer. What a lesson in compassion.

The kids departed for home on a Saturday and Judy and I went to church the next day for what would be the last time she would be able to attend with me. As we sat in a "crying room" we were joined by a young couple with their four-month old daughter, a blessing in itself. The most poignant moment during the service came as we sang four particular words in a worship song, "Joyous victory amidst strife." It is so amazing that believers in Christ as their Lord and Savior can actually take joy in otherwise desperate times, simply due to knowing that this time on earth is so short relative to everlasting life and boundless joy in the presence of God.

Consider the promise God makes to us in Isaiah 46:4:

> Even to your old age and gray hairs
> I am he, I am he who will sustain you.
> I have made you and I will carry you;
> I will sustain you and I will rescue you.

WHAT IS MAN?

What is man anyway, that God should bother to refine us? And what does the scriptural phrase, *refined by fire*, really mean? First of all, the phrase itself has its metaphoric roots in the process of refining silver. When silver ore is heated to a liquid form, the impurities–which are lighter than the silver–float to the top of the mix. This waste–or so-called dross–has no value and is skimmed off, rendering the silver virtually (99.9%) pure.

As the Old Testament prophet Isaiah called the nation of Judah back to God and prophetically spoke to them of God's offering salvation through the Messiah, he explained something of God's refining fires. God did not mince His accusing words: "Your silver has become dross" (Isaiah 1:22). And furthermore, concerning the problem itself, He said, ". . . I will thoroughly purge away your dross and remove all your impurities" (Isaiah 1:25).

What does this mean? God promised to refine His people similarly to the way metal is purged. That process involves the use of lye in a smelting pot. Interestingly, this involves a process of melting the metal and skimming off the impure dross until the worker can actually see his own image in the liquid metal. In other words—as the NIV commentary points out—we must be willing to submit to God, allowing Him to remove our sin so that we might reflect His image.

When the Lord refines us through trials–read the word "refines" as "fire"—He is purifying us. The question I pose is, what is man that God would even *bother* refining us? What else except that He loves us. But with that love He also commands us to share the message of

His Kingdom with others. In Romans 11:32 we are told that "God has bound all men over to disobedience so that He may have mercy on them all." And even though the Jews neglected the mission of being the source of God's blessing to the Gentiles, God blessed the Gentiles anyway through the Jewish Messiah. That's an extra-credit lesson in that so, too, are "all believers called to bring hope to our time." This highly instructional Bible lesson would become the purpose of my *New Day* newsletter, begun in November of 2005, only weeks after Judy's passing.

Both the lessons and God's refining fires continued to rush at me with each passing day, although I did not often see them coming. As I got up one morning and was having my usual breakfast of cold cereal and juice I could hear Judy's racking coughs via the room monitor. Suddenly, I burst into tears as the developing implication struck me once more full in the face. I got up and went to my prayer chair and spoke to God about my plight, asking Him what I should do. I reiterated that I had complete trust in Him, and as I did so His answer was instantly in my head: "If you trust in Me, then that is all you need, even if you don't understand." I had been carrying so much dross I couldn't see my own face through my tears, let alone His.

DREADED PLANNING

One afternoon I told Judy I had some errands to run. What I didn't tell her was that one of them was a visit to the funeral home. As the funeral director and I went over details of what would be involved he quoted me a price for services and burial. I gasped. He and I went to look at the plot area. As we did so the thought came to me, "Why such a show for things that will be placed underground only to deteriorate with time?" The body was not Judy. Her body was merely a vessel for her soul. Only her soul, or spirit, would proceed to heaven. And at His Second Coming she would be given a new and perfect body. Therefore, what need did she (or I) have for the body that would be shed sooner or later?

I remarked that I supposed the cost of cremation would be some less than for burial. He responded matter-of-factly with, "Less than half." Judy and I had on more than one occasion years earlier discussed cremation, so that point would not be a problem for her. My mother, on the other hand, had told me more than once that if I had her cremated she would come back to haunt me. I suppose that was in part due to her experience of having cared for me for so long in conjunction with the third-degree leg burns I had suffered as a seven-year old.

I was concerned with what God has to say on the matter of cremation. What confused me was a statement I had recently heard by a popular Christian radio talk show host. His statement had been that cremation did not point towards resurrection. I called Mike at the church. He assured me that since God will be making us into "new creations" at judgment time anyway, it doesn't matter if we are ashes or bone; i.e., buried or burned. That's what I wanted to hear, and when I broached the subject with Judy she was in full agreement.

I had been regularly going to the health club and my friend, Bob, had often been joining me for my swimming workout. One day, something quite unexpected happened. For all my prayers and witnessing, Bob seemed determined to remain separated from God, certainly so from the saving grace of Jesus Christ. He was a man of few words and even fewer emotions. We shared much and I happened to mention that I hadn't had a paycheck in months, although I was receiving Social Security. He immediately said, "I could let you have four or five thousand dollars, if you need it."

Here was a man who acknowledged God but not His Son, yet always seemed interested in helping those in need. He was a good man but he simply didn't understand his need for salvation. Since Bob would come to an untimely death within a year of that time it is important to me now to know that if he were *ever* going to come to walk with the Lord, God would know that and take it into consideration. I thankfully demurred his generous offer, but my prayers that night were that the Lord might soften the heart of this friend who had just sacrificially offered to help us.

Let me end this section on a lighter note. One morning following a night when Judy's coughing had been quite severe she told one of our daughters-in-law in a phone discussion that just as she had been coughing so harshly she noticed that her sputum looked peach-colored. Judy was immediately concerned about that but then quickly realized something else. The white tissues she was drawing from the Kleenex box had merely gotten down to the "signal" peach-colored tissue. It was time to replace the box!

THE JOY OF WITNESSING

It was toward the end of June of 2004 when early one Sunday morning I was suddenly overcome with physical distress and spiritual forlornness. To get some relief I went upstairs to check on Judy. As I sat with her, rubbing her arms and back I tried to keep her from seeing me weep. She comforted me and said, "I'll be all right. And it's time for you to go to church." Minutes later, as I was shutting down my computer in preparing to leave, I overheard her spontaneous prayer over the monitor. She was praising God and making fervent supplication for me and for our families, as well as for her prayer list of friends and strangers alike. Yet another testimony by Judy.

On another day, after Judy had been up for a short outing and after we finished enjoying our "low-calorie" cheeseburger-fries-and-malted milk shake lunch, we stopped by a drug store for some supplies. As we checked out at the cash register the high school-aged clerk noticed my cross. He said, "That looks like a Star of David overlain on the cross itself." I said, "Thank you," and turning to Judy I added, "my wife gave it to me."

He said, "What is that all about?" Delighted at his question I responded with, "We're Gentiles, but with a heart for the Jewish people." Continuing, I said, "You know, many Jews believe in Jesus as the Jewish Messiah and that He came to earth in human form just as it was prophesied in the Hebrew Scriptures." The young man said he was very interested in knowing more. The next day I dropped off some literature for him and e-mailed a Hebrew Christian high school friend of mine at the same nearby school, asking him to follow up, which he promptly did. What a double treat we enjoyed that particular day.

THE PRIVILEGE OF BEING HELPED

Our finances were not in good shape as the Summer of '04 reached it's mid-point, only five months after Judy's diagnosis. We were set to begin withdrawing from our modest investment accounts when I took a phone call from church friend Valorie. She said, "For your budget planning purposes I want you to know I will be bringing you a check for a very generous amount next week, contributed by your small men's group. They know you're hurting."

I immediately went into the family room where Judy was sitting and told her the incredible news. She said, "I want to do the same thing you're doing (crying), but I can't or I won't be able to breathe." When Valorie arrived with the check, however, it was for nearly 30% more than the figure she had given us. We were overwhelmed. I will share something more in this regard a bit further on in the book.

Off and on, for something like a total of seven months, Stephen Ministry and Loving Meals brought us meals. In fact, they brought so much food we had to request that those servants of the Lord actually drop us from their attentions every other day to only twice a week. Often, the various providers would bring even more than hot and wonderful meals, things such as fresh flowers and prayers. What comfort and blessings.

The woman whom God presented to me when we were both eighteen years old had become, in her darkest hours at age 66, the single most sanctified person I knew. She first walked the walk, and *then* talked the talk. Contrast that with me, whereas when I finally came to the Lord I talked the talk for some time before I was actually walking it.

When I had first noticed Judy in the crowded halls of our high school in our small Iowa town I was a sophomore and she a junior. I was immediately drawn to her carriage, to her beauty, and to her apparent shyness. She had high cheekbones, the result—I supposed—of her however-small Iroquois Indian heritage. She also had what I considered to be exotic eyebrows. They didn't seem to curve downwards as most women's. Add to that her full lips, jade green eyes, and fashionably upturned blouse collar. I only had eyes for her.

Her Indian heritage seems to have been a precursor to international heritages for our family. Our oldest son married a Philippina. Our youngest son married a first generation Cuban-American. And our daughter and son-in-law adopted our first grandson, a native-born Russian. Most recently, of course, came my loving second wife, Helga, who is German-born and raised. To this international flavor we can also add my heart for Israel and the Jewish people. Beyond these circumstances I am reminded that God admonishes us to quite literally love our neighbors, regardless of blood lines and without regard for a natural affinity for them.

The last of this section's vignettes involves the lawn mowing team I mentioned earlier. In one mid-summer's instant the husband had parts of two fingers severed while working with his lawn mower on a neighbor's yard. He and his wife suddenly appeared at our back door, obviously needing help. While I directed him to plunge his wrapped hand into a bucket of ice water—precisely as cool-hand Judy directed me from the kitchen—and then called 911, I knelt down with him and placed my hand on his back. Judy handed me a wet towel for his forehead as I then held it in place and prayed for him.

While all this was going on Judy prayed that the Father would give her the breath she needed so she could tend to their seven-year old daughter who had come with them to work that day, since school was out for the Summer. Now, recall the extra 30% figure Judy and I received beyond the amount Valorie had told us the MOW group had raised for us. The next day I wrote our lawn team a check for that amount. We are only shepherds of our resources, we are not the owners. Incredibly, they would not accept the money and returned the check to us saying they had all they needed. I had a difficult time accepting that a husband-and-wife team who mowed yards for a living had no need of additional funds, but what a witness they were!

THUMBS UP

Judy was due to take a sleep apnea study. The procedure was to determine if her breathing could be helped artificially. At 5:30 the morning following the all-night procedure at which I accompanied her, we went out to breakfast. I asked her what she was thinking and she said, "I'm asking the Father to give me the strength not to be afraid of this cancer. On a conscious level," she said, "I can handle it, but it would be easy to let my thoughts slip before going to sleep each night, fearing for others and also for what I might miss."

At about dinner time that evening I came upstairs from my lower-floor office and as I did I instantly knew Judy was troubled. She said, "I'm scared," and she fell into my arms, crying. That was the first time I had heard her say those words since the day of her diagnosis. We both cried through our embrace, even as I knew she would have to pay the price for crying through increased difficulty in breathing. She talked about how she didn't want to leave but how most of the pain is borne by those who are left behind. It was almost too much for me. It was yet another refining moment for me as Judy once again quietly demonstrated what is meant by God being more interested in our character than in our comfort.

I took Judy to the hospital to have a "port" put in place for Plan C's intravenous injections of the final-resort drug. The anesthesiologist told us that since she couldn't lie down she would have to have general anesthesia rather than sedation and a local. That also meant she would have to be intubated, and probably kept overnight. None of that was good news.

LIFE'S TOUGHEST LESSONS

Five minutes after she had been taken to the operating room the doctor came out to see me and told me of his and the radiologist's concerns. They were recommending a "pic" line instead of the "port." The alternative procedure would require neither the general anesthesia nor intubation, much less a sleepover. I was suddenly lifted up and asked him about Judy's reaction. He smiled and said, "She's leading the cheering section!"

Thirty minutes later I was allowed into the operating room. As I walked in she was still sitting up on the hospital bed, absolutely radiant in her smile. She immediately flashed me an animated "thumb's up," while giving me a robust "Yes!"

What had been the day's lesson for me? That all of God's teaching to that point of her illness had obviously been for me. As the cartoon character Pogo says, "We are confronted with insurmountable opportunities." Absolutely. Isn't it attitude that allows us the freedom to choose rather than lose? Valorie would write to me after Judy's passing to say, "The biggest thing she taught me is attitude. I want to die with her attitude."

We were discovering that on many days Judy's cancer was not her greatest concern. Instead, trigeminal neuralgia (TN) was often her greatest bogey. For several years she had intermittently suffered from this "icepick-like" pain that ran along the vertical portion of her face through her nose, apparently induced by inflammation along her trigeminal nerve. I didn't know if the current cancer treatment had exacerbated things but the TN had returned with such a vengeance that even high-tolerance-for-pain Judy was suffering greatly..

Things had been piling up for her at about that particular time and my thoughts turned to taking a hard look at the road she was traveling relative to the hoped-for destination. While oncologists are naturally fully committed to treating cancer and potentially saving their patients's lives, figuring out how to live with the physical, mental and emotional side effects of cancer treatment is largely left to the patient. How inadequate it is for me to say that it isn't easy.

In David Whyte's *The Heart Aroused* poem he compares the reality of today with the possibility of tomorrow. Because Judy had to put up with so much I wondered about the option of doing nothing to fight terminal cancer, thus optimizing the quality of the remainder of her life. I brought it up to her but she never gave that choice a second thought. That moment reminded me of what someone has said about life and living: "Life is not measured by the breaths we take, but by the moments that take our breath." All of us are suffering from terminal something, if merely old age.

WHAT KEEPS US KEEPIN' ON?

"Terry, I'm not getting any oxygen," Judy softy called, as she woke me one night only half an hour after having retired for the evening. I nearly panicked at first, but managed to switch her oxygen supply to a portable tank before checking the oxygen concentrator. It was making oxygen, but not delivering it. What had happened? Upon closer investigation I discovered the culprit had been me. I had carelessly mis-threaded the water bottle that provided moisture through the oxygen line. The seal necessary to carry the oxygen through the moisture bottle and back into the line was thereby lost. I re-attached the water bottle. Problem solved.

One day I reluctantly came to the conclusion that I would have to give up participation with my long-time and highly beneficial men's Saturday morning Bible study. I could no longer be gone from home for those several early Saturday morning hours each week. When I told Judy I would have to drop out she shook her head and suggested I arrange to have the meetings held at our home. I called the group's de facto leader to see what he thought about the idea. He polled the group and they approved, and that's what we did.

The Men of the Way (MOW) group thrived in meeting at our home, drawing weekly attendance of between seven and eleven of our twelve active members. During the close of that first meeting at our home I put Judy on the intercom as she thanked the group for their willingness to come to our house to meet. Then she praised God and prayed for the men and their families. I wept openly for the broader implication of her being increasingly home-bound. For the next year and a half MOW met at our home, thanks to Judy.

Later that day she and I discussed what was happening in our lives. The most difficult thing for her to say and for me to hear was, "I think of what I am going to miss with you, with our children and our grandchildren." While she was dismayed at that prospect she had long ago given up her dependency on self-sufficiency. Judy understood that God sometimes allows problems to come into our lives that are greater than our abilities can solve.

What can possibly sustain people at times like these? The Bible's answer is very clear: ones's faith in God and the sure knowledge that our hope for eternal life is guaranteed with our salvation through Christ Jesus. Honestly, where else could one go for comfort through calamity except to our inexplicable sovereign Lord? He remains in control and His commands to pray still stand. Even more, He desires to hear from us! As RBC Ministries puts it in *Our Daily Bread*, "Faith is not demanding what we want; it is trusting God's goodness in spite of life's tragedies."

Billy Graham tells that the most important question we should ask when life turns against us is not "Why?" but "What?" In other words, "What do you want me to do, Lord, given these circumstances?" and "What is God trying to teach me?" The answer is to lean on Him for strength. "Show me your ways, O Lord, teach me your paths" (Psalm 25:4).

I was standing in the Kroger check-out line one day and I heard a fifty-something lady in front of me tell the grocery bagger that she was so mad at the world that one way she deals with her anger is to go out and buy a little something to eat. I was trying to think of something to say that might offer her encouragement when the bagger stepped up to the plate and said, "Why are you so angry?"

She paused and then said it was a long story. He said, "It's okay. You're going to be all right." As she walked away with her single product purchase she said, "Thank you for the encouragement." She had obviously come to the store, not really to buy something, but in the hope that someone might care. As I paid for my groceries my thoughts turned to the bagger. I had seen and spoken to him many times and knew that he was developmentally gifted. "I said, "Good work, Edward." I don't doubt that Judy would have been equally prompted to speak up in encouragement of the lady for I had seen her do that very thing many times; often in elevators, medical offices, building lobbies, and even in grocery store aisles.

At a Stephen Ministry meeting one of my fellow ministers told me he was so moved by one of my updates about Judy's attitude that he read it over the air through his Atlanta DJ radio personality. Another of our Stephen Ministers–herself a training leader—was struggling with a return of her cancer *and* a brain tumor on top of that. She would become one of our strongest supporters, even given the fact that she had undergone something like 30 different surgeries over a period of many years. As Judy so often put it in prayer, "Please, God, I'm not complaining. Others have it so much worse, and you have shown me so many mercies."

During the end of July 2004 I took our daughter to the cemetery to see the custom cremation bench I had recently purchased and had set for her mother and me. It was her turn to be quite emotional. She wanted to do more for us–and they did—but regularly bringing herself and our grandchildren up from Florida to visit was tremendous support in itself.

At the next gathering of MOW I asked each of the men to lay their collective hands on a barber's cloth once used by my maternal grandfather. I prayed that God would use us and the cloth as His vessels for Judy's healing, if it was His will, just as He did with the woman in the crowd who intentionally touched the hem of Jesus' garment. I have referenced that Biblical event a number of times simply because the story was so meaningful to Judy. The men then spent fifteen minutes in open prayer for her.

I spoke on the telephone at length with my youngest brother, bringing him up to date. After the call I cried a little as I told Judy I knew it was likely I would not see him again. He couldn't fly and I did not foresee repeating the trip to Denver I had made only a little over two years earlier. He was fighting end stage emphysema himself and Prednisone was his drug partner. His ever stoic comment about life was, "I didn't treat my body well and now I'm paying for it." I have tried to witness to him many times, trying to be very careful not to, as he would put it, "ram it down his throat." I love him so.

I often listened for Judy via the room monitors as I went about my daily household activities, and sometimes that included overhearing her earnest prayers. They were never: "Heal me, Lord," but were always in praise of Him, thankful that she was in Christ, that He was in her, and that she loved Him with all of her mind, strength, body and spirit.

ONWARD, CHRISTIAN SOLDIERS!

Many times, after I would tell Judy I had been praying especially hard for her, she would say, "He may be healing me right now." She would add, "I like to think my coughing is bringing up the bad cancer cells that my little 'Onward, Christian soldiers' are gobbling up." Positive is as positive does.

We received a letter from the Levines of SNI. They wrote that we were in their hearts and that they were asking for God's mercy and compassion to be poured out on us in greater and greater measure. Aside from their thoughts and prayers they also included a sizeable check for, as they put it, "A token of our love to bless you during these difficult times." Helga and I continue to modestly support the organization–as Judy and I did for many years–in the Levine's efforts to raise up leaders for the Messianic movement, both in the United States and abroad.

Let me add to the above comment on the mercy and compassion the Lord poured out upon Judy and me during our marriage. God gives the things of the Holy Spirit to those who seek Him. More than that, He gives Himself to us. And He tells us to endure, rather than guaranteeing He will rescue us from our tribulation. It is God's delight that married couples not only enjoy the fullness of their lives, but their marriage as well. In the very process of a joyful marriage, couples find the intimacy that helps us in our relationship with the Lord.

God allows those who seek Him to intimately find Him simply because He hides Himself in plain sight. How plainly? We are inborn to seek him, but if we resist that call, we are, sadly, unsaved. No one comes to the Lord through his or her intellect, rather our understanding comes by revelation, which leads to relationship. It is left to us, however, to actually accept God's revelation.

Judy and I led a miraculous life together. Why do I say, "miraculous?" Consider that when two selfish people (we are all selfish, we are all sinners) get together, it is not natural to die to oneself for the sake of the other. Therefore, it was a miracle that we had a wonderful life together, one that lasted through 46 years of marriage. It was William Wilberforce, a member of British Parliament in 1807, who spoke so eloquently of man being an apostate creature, that "he is tainted with sin, not slightly and superficially, but radically, and to the very core of his being." It was thus by the grace of God that Judy and I were able to overcome much–but not all–of our human bent.

Once a year our senior pastor would ask the entire congregation to fast for 24 hours. Fasting has always been difficult for me. Not the fasting of television or some other non-food fast, for I can handle that. I am challenged, however, by giving up two or three square meals in a 24-hour period. I do understand, however, that fasting is not only self-denial realized, but that it also provides a clearer sense of one's relationship with the Father.

How easy it is to become wrapped up in one's own problems. God tells us, however . . . and very clearly . . . that we are to 1) love not only Him, 2) but others as well. These are the two Great Commandments, out of which the other eight flow. Loving and doing for others is the foundation for Christian sanctification. We are always to be sensitive to the needs of those around us. I don't mean to say it's easy. On the contrary, I struggle with it, just as I do with fasting. I love one verse in particular of a poem written by Maya Angelou. It reads, "When I say . . . 'I am a Christian' I don't speak of this with pride. I'm confessing that I stumble and need Christ to be my guide."

I received a distressing e-mail one morning from a good friend at our church. This was someone I had sponsored on the Walk to Emmaus and also brought into our Saturday men's Bible study. Some few years later I was also blessed to be asked to spend time with him in conjunction with several of his mentoring classes as he began studying for his Master of Divinity degree.

The e-mail had to do with the baptism of his oldest daughter in our church's outdoor baptismal pool. The evening of that same Sunday his wife took their two children and left home. He had been guilty of practicing the priesthood of believers by living and preaching to his family of Christ and His crucifixion and resurrection as the only way to salvation. A divorce proceeding would follow in time, but he went on to say in his e-mail that in the meantime they were separating and he was moving out of their house. I shared the news with Judy and she cried with me. I asked her if I could invite this true Christian soldier to spend the night with us and she said, "Of course."

Yet another Stephen Minister stayed to visit for a few minutes as she brought us a meal. This time our visitor was a friend whose doctor had not yet been willing to say her cancer was "in remission" but that she was really doing quite well. The three of us talked about both Judy's and her similar cancers and treatments. Ironically, Judy's and my friend would later become the real estate agent who would not only sell both my house in Roswell and Helga's in Woodstock, but also find us the perfect house we would buy together at the time we were to be married.

STRENGTH TO COMFORT OTHERS

Many times I prayed for God to give me the strength to comfort our children as I could plainly see that Judy's health continued to deteriorate. The fact is they comforted Judy and me more often than we comforted them. Our youngest son and his wife, even in the midst of both of their jobs and challenging home remodeling projects, regularly made their way to our house. Our son called almost every night through all the months of his mother's illness. She so looked forward to his phone calls.

Our eldest son and his wife visited often also, in spite of her factory night-shift work and our son's continuous troubleshooting travel that often kept him out of town for two and three weeks at a time without a break. Of him, Judy's mother once said–in a dyslexic, but nevertheless comical, statement–in referring to him in his job as a "trouble*maker*." And, although the KWAK family lived 350 miles away, they regularly made time to come up as well as offering frequent telephone and e-mail support.

One day, a woman was sitting next to Judy in the oncologist's chemotherapy room appeared to have no support at hand. We had often observed this sort of thing in the chemo room, but then families do have to work. In this case, however, the woman seemed quite depressed. You can probably guess Judy's advice once she struck up a friendly conversation with her. That's right, she advised her to ask Jesus to take her hand. At this, the woman not only opened up, she also let Judy pray with her.

In an elevator following her treatment that same morning, a UPS delivery man said to her, "I've seen you here before with your little girl-dressed oxygen tank. Does she have a name?" Judy was delighted to answer his question, saying, "Yes! It's RAWBi, an acronym my husband gave her made up of the first letter of each first name of the four females in our children's families." Then she added the punch line, "As you can see by her cross, she's a Christian." One of my prayers that night was this: "Lord, how is Judy going to continue witnessing to Your glory if she isn't returned to health in this life?" Oh, Lord, I thank you for your grace, but I will need it yet again . . . today.

SHARING

I recently heard a Christian talk-radio personality answer a tough question about whether or not he liked all the people he was supposed to love. He said they were two different elements; that regardless of whether or not he liked someone, he could still love them. How is that? Because loving others has to do with being available to attend to them according to their needs. I bought into that but have since adopted a slightly different attitude. Admitting to not liking someone flies in the face of our admonishment to "love your neighbor." Who is my human reference model for this position? That four-lettered person, Judy, whose name means "praised of the Lord." In spite of what I just wrote about my position on the matter, I don't mean to say this is an easy lesson for me.

For several weeks I had been rehearsing before Judy two upcoming thirty-minute seminar talks. I had included some comments about how our two very different walks with the Lord had converged. Not only had I not come to a saving relationship with Jesus Christ until the age of 58, but once I had, Judy's long-existing faith began growing by leaps and bounds. At one point she asked me to whom I had turned whenever I needed help. I was embarrassed to say that before my walk with Him I had nowhere to turn. It was probably for that very reason I suffered through many personal hardships. I was ashamed to realize that during all of our years of marriage—up to the point of my being saved–Judy had assumed I went to God for help and support in times of personal need, just as *she* did. For all the goodness of our marriage for forty of those years we lacked communication with respect to the issue of faith. How had that happened?

That was the one area of our lives where I had shared with her nothing concerning my spiritual beliefs. Why? I had none. Her faith had been strong, if very private, while I simply hadn't developed any. Not only was I desperately in need of walking with the Lord, but both of us needed to be sharing with each other where we were in that regard. How blessed was I that the Lord never let up in pursuing me, as He does every one who has not accepted His free offer.

After a day in which Judy fought her body's request for daytime sleep, I received a surprise e-mail for her from the nurse who had attended to her during her week long stay at Piedmont Hospital several months earlier. This was the person with whom Judy had prayed concerning her interest in starting a prayer chain within her own church. Judy had later provided her with some detailed suggestions on that point. When I gave her the e-mail I couldn't hold back my tears at her reaction. Her eyes widened and brightened as she softly but excitedly called her name. The nurse had begun her prayer chain and was thanking Judy for her leading.

At 3:00 A.M. one morning as both Judy and I struggled to get back to sleep after one of her particularly difficult coughing episodes, I shared with her another call-in I had heard on a Christian radio talk show earlier that day. The caller's wife had passed away after a two-year caring period and he had been in deep mourning for two months. He was mourning such that he could not stop crying, even on the program. His faith remained unshaken, however, but with no children or significant support group he could find no relief from the loss of his wife of 29 years.

I prayed for him several times earlier that day that he would understand the message he had heard from the radio show host about how a past calamity can ruin anyone's future if, after a season of mourning, you can't let God work with you in building a new life. Unknown to me at the time Judy had recorded that same radio program for my personal benefit. This is the woman to whom I was married and committed for 46 years.

Seven months after her diagnosis Judy asked me to write a letter for her to our senior pastor. Here are excerpts from that letter: "Even though I have not been able to attend services since Terry's Stephen Ministry commissioning in mid-May, due to my immune deficiency vulnerability to large groups, I get to read or hear your messages. I can imagine your delivery since I know your voice, gestures, and mannerisms (most of which, Terry humorously says, he assumes I think are flattering).

"I want you to know that I long ago surrendered all to Him and thus have joy each and every day, as well as a loving family and the many friends in the body of Christ who are seeing me through this. There is simply not enough time for me to thank God for all of His tender and unrelenting mercies, not the least of which is His blessing in bringing Terry and me together for the forty-eight years since we met at age eighteen.

"I particularly want to tell you that the single most helpful blessing I have experienced these past seven months has been the ability, by the grace of God, to reach out on demand to figuratively touch the fringe of the Messiah's garment and ask for Him to hold my hand."

BY THE GRACE OF GOD

More than one oncologist had told us that survival of Judy's type of inoperable lung cancer was as little as six months. In the end she passed that mark more than three times over. For much of that time, however, she was on oxygen 24/7 and with a cough that sounded like the engine of the sorry '57 Nash Rambler we once owned. She also felt puny much of that time, and yet she continued to find more and more for which to be thankful.

I offer the above in contrast to what I am about to write. On September 14, 2004 I asked myself in my journal, "What happened yesterday?" I wrote in answer that I had displayed several unbecoming fits of irritation at some minor happenings. Worse, Judy had witnessed one of them. That, in itself, had caused her to tear up, commenting that she felt so guilty over causing me distress. How flawed am I to have brought on such a reaction from my beleaguered loved one?

Judy's cancer appeared to be taking on a new dimension at that time. I thank God I could not know her appointed time was only one year away. Her cough had become unrelenting. To hear her cough would bring tears to my eyes. I prayed for her continuously. Yet, we both took heart in the value of our salvation and trust in Him for we knew He had a plan for her, "a plan not to harm her, but to prosper her." Some might say, "Well, that didn't happen." But who are we to measure life in its short term when God has given us the promise of everlasting life?

Author Bill Crowder has said, "In the pain and struggle of living without answers, we can always find comfort in our heavenly Father." Consider this anonymous prayer:

> Not ours to know the reason why
> Unanswered is our prayer,
> But ours to wait for God's own time—
> To lift the cross we bear.

On one particular visit to our oncologist, we made a special request. We asked if Judy could take a chemotherapy break of a couple of weeks without putting her at further risk. Our hope was this would allow her to regain some strength. In addition, hurricane Ivan was about to made its dramatic incursion into the Florida panhandle and would surely rip its way northeast to Atlanta for a very unwelcome visit. If things should happen that way we suspected we might have a price to pay.

Within a few hours of our return from the doctor's office our home power went out. It had been three years since I last tested our Y2K-installed and hard-wired generator. The ground-saturating rains suddenly breached our outside entrance basement stairwell, threatening to flood our carpeted basement floor. With a neighbor's help we bailed and water-vacuumed off and on for hours. Through it all—thanks to God's grace and the heretofore unneeded Y2K generator—we had heat, light, and power, not only for Judy's oxygen machine but also power for keeping the water at bay.

It was time to get out my monthly Judy update and newsletter. What follows are excerpts from that newsletter message. Equally important were some very different written responses I received from three friends: a Gentile believer, a Gentile seeker, and a secular Jew. They follow the message.

WHAT AWAITS ME AFTER DEATH?

One question I believe has occurred to every living person in history is this: "What awaits me after death?" I certainly don't have any more insight into answers than what is provided in the Bible, but Jesus' assuring words in John 11:25-26 are overflowing, not only with hope, but with promise: "I am the Resurrection and the Life. He who believes in Me will live, even though he dies; and whoever lives and believes in Me will never die."

Even though I die, I will yet live! What better hope than that? Exactly what are we to make of this? Here is what the Bible tells us: When you and I die we will depart this physical existence for a spiritual one in God's presence. We call that Heaven. And when we are judged it will have nothing to do with either our good works or whether our decision to accept His gracious offer of salvation came early or late in life.

Those in Christ will be given a new physical body on earth and will reside in the presence of God throughout the rest of eternity. Interestingly, we know that those who rejected Him will also be given a physical body and gain everlasting life. The significant downside to Plan B, however, is that it will not be in the presence of God, but in some tortured state we refer to as Hell.

I believe Isaiah 59:2 (NIV) is describing our spiritual death, which comes at the end of our physical life span and he is bemoaning our lack of communion with God; i.e., separation from Him. The prophet puts it this way: "But your iniquities have separated you from your God; your sins have hidden his face from you, so that he will not hear." Whether Israel of the Old Testament or you and I today, sin offends our holy God and separates us from Him. People who die unrepentant—their sin unforgiven—separate themselves eternally from God. And that is surely Hell.

What is the remedy? How can one possibly avoid such punishment since good works alone will in no way avail us of salvation? Scripture provides the answer in 1 John 2:23 (JNT): "Everyone who denies the Son is also without the Father, but the person who acknowledges the Son has the Father as well." David Stern, in his JNT Commentary illustrates this further in reminding us that "trusting in God necessarily implies trusting in the Son."

Many people (both Jews and Gentiles) claim to "trust" in God, but don't define "God" as the one who sent his Son, Christ Jesus, to atone for their sins by His death. Those who define their "trust" as such are not trusting in the God who created all, but in a god shaped by themselves. Paul speaks of this trust as always being in the God who was, and is, and will be: the God of the Bible.

We look to Paul's letter to the Romans in Rom. 5:12-21 (NIV) for exactly how this works. Now bear with me because these three paragraphs together have been called one of the greatest theological passages in the Bible.

"Therefore, just as sin entered the world through one man, and death through sin, and in this way death came to all men, because all sinned—for before the law (Torah) was given, sin was in the world. But sin is not taken into account where there is no law. Nevertheless, death reigned from the time of Adam to the time of Moses, even over those who did not sin by breaking a command, as did Adam, who was a pattern of the one to come.

"But the gift is not like the trespass. For it the many died by the trespass of the one man, how much more did God's grace and the gift that came by the one man, Jesus Christ, overflow to the many! Again, the gift of God is not like the result of the one man's sin. The judgement followed one sin and brought justification. For if, by the trespass of the one man, death reigned through that one man, how much more will those who receive God's abundant provision of grace and of the gift of righteousness reign in life through the obedience of the one man.

"The law was added so that the trespass might increase. But where sin increased, grace increased all the more, so that, just as sin reigned in death, so also grace might reign through righteousness to bring eternal life through Jesus Christ our Lord."

We can actually reduce the incredible hope and wonderful promise of these verses–although it is simplistic to do so–to merely six words: Death through Adam, life through Christ.

I recently read in a Salvation Army article that all of this reveals one of the great misconceptions about faith: "The common view is that faith is all about having the correct information and physical evidence about God. Then and only then would we believe completely." Jesus told one such person who, after he died, realized the error of his ways and pleaded with Abraham to send back a righteous man named Lazarus, who had also recently died. He was certain that an eyewitness returning from the dead could speak to his five brothers and convince them of the truth. But Abraham said, "If they do not listen to Moses and the prophets, they will not be convinced even if someone rises from the dead" (Luke 16:31 NIV). Sadly, that is the case for many yet today, for Jesus Himself rose.

Some polls reflect that as many as 80% of the people in the United States believe in God, but what does expressing faith mean without a full commitment to His word and His way of life? Even demons believe that and tremble with fear. So then, what *does* await us after death? Well, that depends entirely upon your relationship with Christ *before* you die. There is no second chance following death.

Some people ask, "Will Christ actually return to earth some day?" Judy had no doubt because of her faith. 1 Thessalonians 4:16 gives us the definitive answer about the coming again of Christ: "For the Lord himself will come down from heaven, with a loud command, with the voice of the archangel and with the trumpet call of God, and the dead in Christ will rise first."

Yet, it is not enough to know of Christ's certain return, for those who have rejected His way of salvation through Jesus Christ will be judged. The best news ever to be given is that we don't have to give up this life for eternity without being in the presence of God. And that news is guaranteed through our commitment to Christ. If you haven't made that commitment I don't recommend waiting to age 58 to do so–as I did–for tomorrow is given to no man.

THREE NOT OF A KIND

So what did three respondents have to say about the above newsletter which accompanied my seventh-month Judy update? "God bless you," one letter began, and then added, "Thanks for sending me this. It was what I needed to 'hear' at this particular time. God is good and His timing is perfect."

Then we received this from a second recipient: "It was nice reading about death and what it can mean if you believe in Jesus Christ. I would very much like to come by your house for one or two of your Saturday morning Bible studies."

But then there was also the third letter, which read, "While we are eager to hear how you and Judy are doing and how we might be of help, I'd rather not receive e-mails such as the one prompting this response." To reader number three I could only e-mail him that I would respect his request. I did add, however, that, "In spite of your not having embraced your own Messiah, as is true of many Jewish people, most Christians love the Jewish people. And we do so whether or not you or any particular Jewish person *ever* comes to accept the Messiah. That's because without the Jewish people there would be no Christianity."

Without Christ, what would be the purpose of life? A noted scientist has said, " Man is no more than an accidental fungus." The Bible, however, tells us that we were not only made in His image but that we were made to last forever. As Rick Warren puts it, "One day my heart is going to stop, and that will be the end of my body–but not the end of me." The body is merely the vehicle which houses the soul. We are not our body. Until we realize that we were made by and for God, life simply isn't going to make sense.

Judy knew this truth and thus trusted God for when it came time for her to depart her body. She and I discussed the book of Job on this subject many times. We found several of Job's verses to be particularly relevant to the transiency of this life on earth. They are found in chapter 14: 1-2, 10: "Man born of woman is of few days and full of trouble. He springs up like a flower and withers away; like a fleeting shadow, he does not endure . . . man dies and is laid low; he breathes his last and is no more."

But, as the next to the last chapter in 1 Corinthians confirms, that is hardly the end. In fact, not only is death not the end of life, but it is the gateway to everlasting life. "Where, O death, is your victory? Where, O death, is your sting? . . . Thanks be to God! He gives us the victory through our Lord, Jesus Christ." Judy and I often talked about this truth.

IT IS TRULY ALL ABOUT TRUST

On September 23, 2004 our youngest son began to help me with a critical house project, converting half of our large finished basement room from Judy's former office to a much more useable church group meeting space. That had been Judy's suggestion at the time the Bible study group moved from the church to our home.

With Judy's subsequent inspection and approval of the project I then undertook a much more difficult challenge. I drove her to the cemetery in Roswell. My intention had been to merely drive by and point out where our cremation bench had been recently installed. She wanted to see it up close, however. I was nervous about how she might react and I quietly asked the Lord for help. To Judy I said, "I planned to have an epitaph engraved on the bench seat for each of us, but I only knew for certain what yours would be. I'll do mine later." I was tremendously relieved that she approved of the following, which was engraved on the top of the granite bench above her name and birth date:

SHE WAS JOYFUL ALWAYS:
PRAYED CONTINUALLY;
GAVE THANKS IN ALL CIRCUMSTANCES,
FOR THIS WAS GOD'S WILL FOR HER IN CHRIST JESUS.

It would be exactly one year from that date that my gentle Judy would be called home by God. That same night, after a jarring coughing episode she said, "I thank God that I am not in serious pain. He is so merciful." Remembering our earlier reading from

Job I compared her attitude with his, whose cry from the rubble of personal calamity rang out: "Though He slay me, I will trust Him."

SWEET SOUNDS

Who would think a plan would be needed for climbing stairs? Because Judy no longer had the lung capacity to easily climb the stairs from the main floor to our second floor bedroom, we devised a plan whereby I would assist her as she climbed four steps at a time. At each four-step interval I would wait at her side for fifteen seconds before she continued climbing. For a while she could do this and arrive at the top step without being breathless. After some months, however, this routine required thirty-second rest periods.

A friend and former long-time customer of ours sent us an amazing e-mail. In it she offered "to come and sit with Judy, do household chores, run errands, whatever," adding that it would be her privilege. Our friend lived and ran her business 150 miles away in South Carolina.

During the Fall of 2004 and during part of the Winter of 2005, I began regularly pitching horseshoes on the backyard court I had constructed. I needed some way to both exercise and compete (at least with myself) so that I wouldn't have to go to the health club and leave Judy for several hours at a time. For months to follow I would almost daily pitch from 50 to 200 shoes, always with the goal of increasing my ringer percentage. Judy could always hear the clang of steel-on-steel and thus know that I was nearby.

Not often enough to suit me I would watch in hopeful anticipation as the two and a half pound piece of steel left my right hand to fly through the air in a low arc towards its target forty feet away. At the other end of the court, only fourteen inches of the six-foot steel rod's total length protruded above the Georgia dirt. The one-inch diameter steel stake leaned three inches forward from the vertical, awaiting arrival of the three-quarter turn of a horseshoe.

Such a shoe arrived (about 30% to 40% of the time) parallel to the ground with a shuddering clank–caulk down and face open– directly below the top of the stake. As steel would grate past steel in the shoe's split-second drive to the orange-colored dirt and sand pit below, I would pump a fist in gleeful satisfaction. On those occasions—when I had managed a ringer–my thought was, "that is the sweetest sound I've ever heard."

A sweet sound indeed, but surely not as sweet sounding as the regular greetings of our three married offspring and their dear spouses and children, come to see us. And I knew the sound was not nearly as sweet as the Gospel music refrain, "Jesus, Jesus, Jesus, Sweetest Sound I know." But there was one sound sweeter to me than any of those. I heard it often, for every time I entered the house after having finished my practice in the pits, Judy would simply say, "How did you do, sweetheart?"

One day I took her to get her annual flu shot at a pharmacy. As we waited in line to obtain the pharmaceutical form I asked a question of someone also in line. He then noticed the Star of David on the cross around my neck and said, "Covering your bases, huh?" I gently replied, "Not at all, my Lord is a Jewish carpenter."

On our only granddaughter's twelfth birthday KWAK had been visiting us from Jacksonville for a few days, as we all gathered for her birthday party. She asked to have her party at our home. Nearly the entire immediate family attended, and after polishing off a beautifully decorated horse head-shaped cake (but with no gift of either a horse or a pony), we danced in our kitchen. Abigail had been taking ballroom dancing lessons and I asked her to dance. Almost immediately after our first dance our six-year old grandson got up and asked his grandmother to dance. Judy responded with tears in her eyes, saying, "I would love to dance with you, Karsten, but I'm not able. Thank you so much for honoring me."

On one of our regular weekly chemotherapy visits to our oncologist we were sitting in the waiting room. Judy could see that the only other person in the room was a young woman. She was wincing, apparently in pain. Judy greeted her and asked if she could pray with her. The woman's answer was an immediate, "Oh, yes."

As we left the doctor's office and got into the elevator, a man about our age wheeled in a woman—presumably his wife—who was obviously in pain. The woman remarked on how cute Judy's oxygen tank looked, dressed as a little girl. The moment the elevator door closed Judy asked if she could pray for her and the response was, "Oh, my. Yes." It was all I could do to fight back my tears for this wife of mine who always thought first of others, even as she would be visiting the doctor for treatment of her cancer. Was I beginning to understand the concept of one's being shaped and developed—pruned—for the purpose of producing more fruit, at least as it applied to me? I may as well have been renamed "Prunes."

In late October of 2004 I mailed our eighth month Judy update/newsletter to family and close friends. Of the many messages of support we received, the response that touched us the most was from a former business customer of ours in Florida. Her sweet words were, "I asked God to speak to me today and cannot thank you enough for your letter of faith, hope and encouragement, which arrived only hours later."

EARN, SAVE, GIVE, PRAY

Only a week or so before Judy's diagnosis she had told me that since we had just retired she was now ready to become involved with Mt. Pisgah's "A Beacon of Hope" (ABOH) ministry in sharing and caring for girls and women with crisis pregnancies. She had felt so moved by the plight of unwanted babies, but her illness came upon her at nearly the same time and thus she would then not be granted the opportunity to do anything about her plans. A commemorative brick now rests in the ABOH's new building's courtyard from Helga and me in Judy's honor.

As Judy and I sat down to discuss our church-giving for 2004-2005 we marveled at how God had provided in making it possible for us to maintain the same dollar level of giving as the year before, even though our business income had dropped significantly. And then we made an even greater discovery. The previous year we had tithed on income *after* business expenses, while during our first year in retirement we were tithing on our *gross* income. In other words, we were truly giving to the Lord of our first fruits rather than from leftover fruit. And still He provided.

Interestingly, almost exactly a year later, after Helga and I had married, we participated in a financial Bible study with three other believing couples from our church. The focus in that Crown series was to learn how the Bible teaches us to manage not merely our finances, but *all* of our resources. The bottom line is that it is wise to earn all we can . . . so long as we also save all we can . . . and give all we can. But to fully understand all of the preceding it is also necessary to pray.

Back in real time, during one busy afternoon as Judy was finishing the balancing of our checkbook, a friend came to visit us. The three of us talked about a number of things as we spent an hour together and closed with prayer. At about 6:00 P.M. another friend came to share dinner with us and visit with me about personal issues, including my sugar addiction and his struggles with a several-year old divorce, his prayer life and smoking. We, too, closed our meeting with prayer. I mention these two visits because believers are clearly told to not only spend time in church but to also give of ourselves time in fellowship and prayer with other believers in both small groups and one-on-one. Christianity does not thrive in a vacuum.

LIFELINES

One day, during what we thought would be a routine chemo treatment at the doctor's office, the nurses could not draw blood through Judy's PICC line, even after repeated attempts. "Her blood has clotted," one nurse said, adding, "We'll try to thin the blood by pushing some Heparin into the line." After two tries, that didn't work either. One of the technicians said he was praying for Judy and the nurse responded with, "You're going to have to pray a little harder."

Still no success. The nurse then said, "The only other thing we can do is try using a much stronger thinner, but that will take a while. If that doesn't work we'll have to schedule her for surgical implantation of a new PICC line in the other arm." That upset both of us and I then prayed with her. We waited an hour for the blood to thin and suddenly, we could see beautiful red blood filling the lifeline and we said, almost in unison, "Hallelujah!"

Later that morning, after the chemo treatment had been completed, I went to get the car from the parking garage in order to collect Judy. As I was pulling up to the lobby I saw her talking to a stranger. I motioned to her but she put up her forefinger in a signal that she would be right there. As she joined me a few minutes later I said, "You were praying with her, weren't you?" She said, "Yes, but that's between the two of us and God."

Once, during a visit by one of the two-woman housecleaning teams that had been coming to help me on a biweekly basis, something special happened. I had gone to do some grocery shopping while the helpers were at our house. When I returned, Judy told me that when she had inquired of one of them about her family the woman shared her concern for her young son, whom she was raising alone. He had just begun smoking and the mother told Judy she had a family history of cancer, past and present. Judy prayed with her and the woman cried. Judy reminded her that God performs miracles all the time, even "in the twinkling of an eye," and for her to remain hopeful. The fact is that God heals through medicine, miracles, and resurrection.

IOWA COMES TO GEORGIA

Judy's two younger sisters and their husbands arrived from Iowa for our much-anticipated week-long visit with them. I met them at the airport with a large, black marker-inked poster I had made. On it I had drawn both a bold question mark and a symbolic fence post. The symbols were supposed to suggest their last names: Riddle and Postma. Unfortunately, they saw me before they saw the sign. The youngest sister, Rusti, later said she "got it." All the artistic-minded middle sister, Kaye, had to say was she thought my depiction of the post was pitifully poor. In any event, their visit was more than a simple reunion. It was the final, joyous, in-person lifeline the three of them would share. Everyone knew it, but no one spoke of it.

The sisters also surprised us with a check from their father for Judy. He had recently helped each of the other girls in a similar fashion and wanted to be certain Judy got her share. Only two days before I had told Judy we would have to pull some money from our investment funds in order to meet the month's obligations. How merciful He is.

Shortly after Judy's family had arrived at our home I prayed about how to best witness to them. Wouldn't you know that when Martin and Betty came over to show everyone a video they had made of their house-remodeling, the same CD contained Judy's and my renewal of our faith-focused wedding vows six months earlier. And that was topped by the video of my Stephen Ministry commissioning!

When the afternoon came to drive the sisters and their husbands to the Atlanta airport for their return to Iowa, we did so with joy for their visit, but sadness for its conclusion. We both felt blue the rest of the day, and that evening we had a short cry together. Judy said, "I tried to be strong, but I will so miss my sisters." By that she meant she knew she would never see them again in this life.

FAITHFUL FRIENDS

Following one of Judy's increasingly frequent and worsening coughing spells she seemed to be over it and flashed me her trademark thumb's up and v-fingered signs. I asked her what she would like to do. She responded almost immediately with a broad smile and three little words that meant so much to her comfort, "Wash my hair!" Wow. What an honor for me.

After a routine chemo treatment and lunch at our favorite buffet restaurant we happened to sit near a table with the lady who owned the barber shop I frequented. Two of her associate barbers were with her, all three of which were believers. The owner bothered to come over to our table to tell us that Judy was in their prayers.

On more than one day I was beset with not only Judy's needs, but my aging mother's as well. On a day when I was supposed to take my mother to a dermatologist to have her angioma biopsied Judy was feeling so poorly that she made a rare request, asking me not to leave for the three hour trip it would require to see to my mother. I debated whom to call for help. I opted for my mother's assisted living facility's head nurse. Only the week before she had very specifically told me she would be glad to help if she could. She knew full well my situation at home so I didn't doubt her sincerity. That marvelous lady-of-faith not only took my mother for her appointment, and then stayed with her, but afterwards took her to McDonald's and bought her a milkshake! "What you did for the least of my children, you did for me."

On Thanksgiving weekend of 2004, with KWAK visiting, Judy did not want to spend the three hours necessary to go into the downtown Atlanta oncologist's office to have her dressings changed. She wanted to invest that time with our visiting out-of-town family. I had mentioned this to Kevin before they left Jacksonville and he said he would bring the necessary supplies in order to flush the line and change the dressing himself. Judy was so happy to hear that the mountain would come to her.

That night, as I lay in my bed next to Judy in her sleep-chair I was seized with emotion and cried silently, but in such volume that I could not stem the tears with either my hands or my bed sheet. The next morning all Judy said was, "I hope you have a better night tonight, Teh-wee!"

Judy's last Thanksgiving holiday in this earthly life was so wonderfully spent. All of our children and their spouses and children, plus my mother, were present. All except for Jason, that is. He was trapped in Houston on an emergency trouble-shooting trip for his company that caused him to miss the holiday altogether. He got home a day later, both disappointed and tired since he had slept only two hours in the previous 48, missing the holiday with his wife, family, and especially his mother.

The Saturday morning before KWAK were to depart, our son-in-law sat in with the MOW group for our Bible study. The group enjoyed asking him questions about the Messianic movement in which he and our daughter have active membership and responsible roles in a Jacksonville congregation. Afterward, he and I had a chance to talk and we spoke about my concerns should it become necessary to call 911, as well as the benefit to using at-home hospice. I knew Judy had questions about the latter, in particular. He said he would talk with her later and allay her concerns, which he did.

Before everyone left, Kevin scribbled a note and left it for me, along with a check for not only a replacement water heater for the one which had failed during their visit, plus a replacement powder room commode, and even enough for a new convection stove! The note said that he and Wendi had talked it over and justified their generosity through having received an unexpected bonus the past month. Surely it must have been intended for this purpose. From whom much is given much is expected. Their gift of hospitality has been demonstrated over and over, not only for family, but for friends and strangers alike. How blessed were Judy and I to be given three wonderful offspring and end up with six loving people, each of whom affectionately called us "mom" and "pop."

ABUNDANT BLESSINGS

In the process of witnessing Judy's courageous fight against her inoperable lung cancer I was sometimes frustrated by my own inability to address others' simple questions as to how she was doing. One thing was very clear to me, however. Through all of her trials she never failed to praise God as she would talk to Him throughout her day and thank Him for all the incredible blessings of life. In other words, while her body was failing, her Spirit was not.

Many simply do not understand that we must not despair even though we suffer. To paraphrase Christian writer Oswald Chambers: "If God has made sweet the cup from which we drink, we can no less drink from it if He has made it bitter." Chambers went on to further develop his point: "Now, given this bitter-sweet realization–along with the fact that the world largely rejects the Savior–should we still be about His work? Of course! It is as He told us it would be."

Some people say of their lives, "God just wants me to be happy." Well, we may think that, but the truth is that God wants us to be obedient. With obedience will come many feelings, very likely including happiness, but especially joy. Judy had great peace and joy in her life in spite of––for example–the fact that for 570 consecutive days she did not once lie down for fear of choking to death. She substituted peace for complaint. Her joy came because she did her best to be obedient. How different I used to be in that regard. God let me struggle to the point that I finally called out to Him for help. It was only then that I learned what Judy had known all her life, that happiness springs from joy.

As I pondered these things of faith I came across a very interesting article by the noted Dr. Allen Blair. In the following commentary I quote from it with express permission. Dr. Blair begins his point with this intriguing and relevant story: A Japanese express train was racing toward Tokyo from a mountain village. Most of the passengers in the first-class coach were concentrating on the problem of maintaining life in the midst of their population explosion. A university freshman who was seated next to a missionary had his mind on religion. "Tell me," he asked the missionary, "What is the difference between Christianity and other religions?"

"Christianity is not a religion," replied the missionary.

The college student was surprised and asked, "How can you, a Christian missionary, say that?" Man searches for religion. Can't man find Him by means of Christianity as well as by any other religion?"

"You are right," said the missionary, "when you say that man seeks God by means of religion. Man has manufactured thousands of religious systems to aid him in his search for God. However, it is not God but man who is lost. Once and for all, God has revealed Himself to man. Salvation has been provided for all who will accept it on God's terms. Religion is vain because through religion man seeks to do what God has already done." What a wonderful and instructional story.

We read in 1 John 5:11 the following: "And this is the witness: God has given us eternal life, and this life is in his Son." Nonbelievers, whether Jewish or Gentile, have actually gone far astray on the issue of the Messiah in opposing the concept of Him being both fully God and fully man.

As Daniel Juster writes on this point in *Israel's Restoration*, "How heartbreaking!" Juster explains–from the Jewish perspective—that nothing is culturally more incorrect and rejected by the Jewish people than the deity of Yeshua (Jesus). Even though the Bible is a very Jewish book, Judaism rejected the possibility that the Son–who is part of the identity of God–could become flesh. This, then reminds us that most Jewish people will not bear the price of embracing Jesus even if the assertion of the New Testament is unmistakable in a Jewish context. As I have stated, I love the Jewish people simply because we Gentiles owe them such a debt of gratitude. But those who have rejected Him are no exception to vanity being everywhere apparent–be it Judaism, Hinduism, Buddhism, or Islam—on the face of man's false religious interpretations.

While Judy and I struggled with the frustration of seemingly not being able to witness as effectively as we would have liked to family, friends, and strangers, we were yet aware that the eternal God, the giver of everlasting life, is continually in search of His sheep who have gone astray. God is always pursuing us through prevenient grace (remember that this is the grace God gives us before we know Him). There never has been and never will be a religious system which can undo the damage done to mankind through sin. It is Jesus, and Jesus only, who can save us. There have been millions of earnest people who have been deceived into thinking that religion saves.

One of the saddest letters-to-the-editor I have ever read appeared in *TIME* magazine several years ago. The reader wrote, "Why should we care about the existence of God, with all the evidence that our interest is not reciprocated?"

The truly sad calamity is that there are many people who go to church regularly who have never experienced a personal relationship with Jesus Christ. I was such a person in my adolescence. They are religious, but lost. We read in John 3:36, "Whoever trusts in the Son has eternal life." Now, if we have received Christ into our life, we are saved. But if we have not received Him, we are lost. Why is that? Quite simply, God paid an enormous price for our salvation. When Christ died on the cross He did so for our sin. He did not die for His own sins for He had none.

True believers will be singing praises unto the One who purchased their right to heaven by the shedding of His own blood. In case you think you can "work" yourself into heaven be reminded that if you were to go to heaven on any other grounds, you would indeed have reason to boast. But no one in heaven will ever be able to boast about putting himself or herself there. The apostle Paul said it for the ages in Ephesians 2:8-9: "For it is by grace you have been saved, through faith–and this not from yourselves, it is the gift of God–not by works, so that no one can boast."

There is only *one* way of salvation. It is not through any particular denomination. It is through faith in Jesus Christ and Jesus Christ alone. He said it very simply: "I am the way, the truth, and the life. No man cometh unto the Father but by me" (John 14:6). I cannot resist the cliche: What part of that don't we understand?

ENTER HOSPICE

Before Judy was admitted to at-home hospice care she and I discussed its implications at great length. For me, the word initially had a dreadful meaning. I didn't understand that it signaled anything but the end of this life. That's why when the word was first mentioned in concert with a specific facility I immediately went there to check it out. It was during that visit that I discovered the difference between in-patient and at-home hospice. The former represents an ending while the latter provides pain management and care for however long.

In late November of 2004 Judy said of her decision not to undergo further chemotherapy, that it was "as if a burden had been lifted from my shoulders." Two critical decisions had been made: 1) to forgo chemotherapy and 2) to accept at-home hospice. It was at that point that I allowed myself for the first time to briefly consider my life after Judy. That process was both emotional and painful because I couldn't share my thoughts with my life's love. All I could really consider was how important it was for me to be a part of our grandchildren's lives.

I needed to talk with someone so I phoned my best friend. Jack lives in Iowa where we both grew up. Over the telephone we discussed our current lives, we talked of the changing events of the past fifty years. A day or so later, when the hospice chaplain came to visit for the first time and then prayed comprehensively with us as she prepared to leave, Judy said, "I know God sent her to see us with this program."

Explaining the critical decisions of the previous few days to our children yielded mixed results. Martin was understandably upset with the implications and questioned the chemo discontinuance. Wendi was quite pleased with the decisions since Kevin had recommended both. We couldn't reach Jason at the time as he was troubleshooting somewhere west of the Mississippi River, out of cell phone range.

When Judy and I retired that evening I asked if she would like to watch television for a bit. She said, "I would rather sit and hold hands and joyously praise the Lord." From then on we made that a nightly happening. When I told her she was my spiritual heroine she patted me on the shoulder and said, "Honey, we're beginning yet another adventure together."

Following communication of our decisions to family and friends we received many supportive return e-mails, including one from a long-time fellow industry multi-line representative. In his e-mail he mentioned Luke 17:11-19 and how only one of the ten lepers healed by Jesus thanked him. Jesus answered the one with, "Were there not ten cleansed? Where are the nine?" My friend's point was not about the nine, but the one, about being both thankful and thanking others.

The third hospice nurse to visit us within the first week was a believer, just as were the first two. Frankly, I don't think hospice work would be well suited to those with lukewarm faith. She explained the benefits and usage of sublingual morphine for shortness of breath, which medication would be regularly employed by us in the coming months. The only trying aspect of that visit came when the nurse said– addressing herself to me—"Let me tell you about our bereavement service for when Judy passes on." I was taken aback and politely cut her off, saying we were focused in another direction. She immediately reversed herself, even sharing with us that she had a cancer client who only that week had suddenly and mysteriously found herself free of her bone, liver and one other cancer! Doctors cannot cure cancer, but God can and sometimes does.

On our eldest son's 39th birthday he and his wife joined us, cake and barbecue in hand. That was the first opportunity I had to take him aside and explain where everything stood. He comforted me by holding and rubbing my arm and then we had a little cry together. That was a first in life for the two of us together and it meant a great deal to me. Judy took great comfort in that circumstance when I later shared it with her.

If you have never had a professional therapist massage your feet you are missing one of life's wonderful little pleasures. Judy loved her first massage therapy treat and I subsequently arranged for her to receive an hour's such attention in our home about every six to eight weeks.

During her first "happy feet" treatment I left the house in order to visit the funeral home for pre-planning beyond the cremation bench itself. My emotions were naturally raw. My thinking was along the lines of, "How can I be doing this alone? We have always shared everything, and now the single most momentous planning event of our lives precluded such sharing." When the funeral home representative asked me which songs I would like for the service I could not respond. All I could manage for a few seconds was to bite my lip before yielding to an unashamed torrent of tears.

Later, I consoled myself with reading from a devotional booklet about death, which said *non*believers in Christ as their Lord and Savior have no hope. Why? Because whatever enjoyment they had in life is gone and there is nothing to which to look forward. But death has a bright side for those who believe. While it is the end of some things we have enjoyed, it is the beginning of a new life that will not only be far better, but will never end.

A few days later a hospice nurse arrived to remove Judy's PICC line. Judy was quite apprehensive, thinking it might be akin to a surgical procedure. The nurse removed the dressing and then applied pressure at the port. She asked if Judy was okay and then simply snapped out the line. Judy broke into a broad smile, saying, "That was it?"

Before long yet another hospice person came to visit. This time it was a 41-year old Hispanic chaplain who had seen duty with the Navy and Marines in Afghanistan. He tenderly prayed with us and as he was about to leave he looked me in the eyes and touched my arm as he asked, "Now, how are *you* doing, Terry?" Until then no one had really asked me that question, and I loosed yet another flood of tears.

JOKING AROUND

I've never seen someone get so much out of a joke as Judy did over one she heard and repeated frequently for nearly six months. She had always claimed she couldn't remember jokes, but this one seemed to stay with her. She took special joy in regaling others with it. I think this may have been special to her because the story is a parallel to how the humble will surely inherit the earth.

Judy's joke: Four people and three parachutes are aboard an airplane with engine difficulties. The first one says, "I'm a heart surgeon and many people are depending upon me for their lives." He grabs one of the chute packs and bails. The second guy says, "I'm a rocket scientist and some have said I'm one of the most brilliant people in the world. Without me the next space shuttle will never leave the ground." With that he also grabs a pack and bails.

The third person is the pastor of a small church and he says to the fourth person aboard—a Boy Scout—"Son, I'm an old man. You take the last parachute." The Boy Scout says, "Thanks, but don't worry, pastor. The smartest guy in the world just jumped out of the airplane with my back pack."

One night, as Judy was particularly beset with a coughing episode that wracked her body for minute after minute, she turned to me and said, "Tomorrow, be certain to make our semiannual life insurance payments." Judy the pragmatist. Once again I found myself beset with tears, although I would turn away in order to spare her my emotion.

The hospice nurse came again on her routine twice-a-week visit and said, "Today, I'm going to demonstrate use of the suction machine." I about had heart failure. The dreaded suction machine! But guess what? It turned out to have an *oral* function, not *nasal*, as I had earlier–but mistakenly— understood. "It's no big deal," she said. " Dentists use this sort of machine all the time." Wow! I had envisioned having to thread a thin tube up Judy's inflamed nose if it came to her not being able to push the secretions out of her mouth. I had to laugh to keep from crying.

Judy wanted me to pick up a few things for her for Christmas at a department store and asked if she could go with me, yet remain in the car. I said, "No, but I'll tell you what. I'll borrow my mother's wheel chair and take you in with me." We looked like a multi-car train as we wheeled in, me pushing Judy in the wheel chair as she pushed RAWBi (the wheeled oxygen tank). We had a wonderful time laughing and traversing the store. We also inadvertently terrorized several customers by my weaving the wheelchair in and out of the aisles. She kept asking me to slow down, but in reading her body language I knew she was having a fine time.

WHAT LIMITS, FORGIVENESS?

Do you remember a time when you might have been so ashamed of something you had done that in your unbelief you thought even God could not forgive you? Fortunately for us God nowhere in His Word presents any evidence for such limits. Even Judas, had he been able to repent of his condemnation of Jesus and ask forgiveness, would likely have had salvation granted him. There is, nevertheless, consequences for anyone's acts of disobedience.

Judy told me on a number of occasions that she often prayed for God to reveal any corner of her life where she needed to either offer or ask forgiveness. Through the last ten years or so of her life she made overt efforts to apologize to anyone she may have inadvertently hurt in her life, as well as cleansing her heart of any lingering unforgiven offense against her.

The Bible is replete with examples of terrible deeds performed by both believers and unbelievers. To mention only two Biblical examples we can turn to Paul and David. These are seen by Paul through his initial zealous persecution of believers in Jesus as the Messiah, and David for his indiscretion with Bathsheba and the subsequent manipulation of the murder of her husband, Uriah. Through confession and repentance both were forgiven their transgressions. They were forgiven, but not absolved. Both would suffer the consequences of their deeds. David would forfeit his infant bastard son's life and Paul would be led to reverse his course and perilously champion the very savior he had persecuted.

What about limits to forgiveness in this day? One indirectly personalized example involved an individual I did not know but also the only church I recall having attended over more than a twenty year period (even if it was for only a few months during 1979). This was the focus of a Delaware, Ohio newspaper account by reporter Susan Kelley, from which this story is built. The church was Old Stone Presbyterian—located only a quarter of a mile from the rural area where we once lived. The person was a 22-year old arsonist by the name of Johnnie Munday, who was raging against God for the injustices and hurt in his early childhood and adolescence. He then committed what he considered the unforgivable sin.

Munday was caught, tried, convicted, and served seven and a half years for his crimes, which included burning down Old Stone and three other Delaware county churches in the same week in 1989. Nine times prior to his acts of arson he had attempted to take his own life, wanting to escape the taunts of his learning-disabled childhood and medical problems which had led to severe depression. He had actually sought God for answers, but when he didn't get them he began to hate God. As his health deteriorated, the pent-up rage of this wheelchair-bound individual manifested itself in an arson spree.

In prison, however, a fellow inmate talked to Munday about God, although he denied Him for a long time to follow. Halfway through his incarceration time, however, he had a near-death experience in which he said Christ appeared to him. "He was suddenly there for me," Munday says. "He revealed Himself to me. All my questions as to why I suffered were answered, because He suffered for me." On December 26, 1995, after asking Jesus into his heart, he said, "I got out of the wheelchair and walked." His comment was, "I had only deserved to die and yet He came to save me."

What Munday had considered his unforgivable sin led him to confession, repentance, and salvation. (These were the elements Judas' crime did *not* include.) But the story doesn't end there. Shortly after his release from prison in 1997 he returned to Old Stone—and in turn to each of the other three churches he had burned(three of the four churches had been rebuilt or restored and the fourth had merged with a sister denominational church). As he addressed the congregations from a simple introduction of "someone who has something to say," members' shocked expressions betrayed their realization as they came to understand who the speaker was.

Munday did not say, "I'm sorry." Rather, he asked for forgiveness. God had forgiven him, but now he was asking men for their forgiveness as well. He would not be disappointed. Johnnie Munday was redeemed and forgiven, although he surely paid a price for his shameful acts, just as Paul and David and countless others have.

A SPECIAL CHRISTMAS

As we began receiving our Christmas season cards, one arrived from our still-youngish postman of many years. It read, "Your thoughtfulness toward me is incredible. It has been my good fortune knowing you throughout the years. Your commitment to each other is such an inspiration to me." How humbling is that? It was Judy who reminded me every year to "put enough gift fast food certificates in the hands of our mail man, as well as the newspaper, and the UPS delivery people."

One night at about 7:30 the door bell rang. As I opened it I judged there were about thirty-five Christmas carolers from church in our front yard. I rushed to get Judy and then helped her onto a kitchen chair I drug into the hallway so she could see them through the glass door. It was quite cold but they sang three carols. As we looked at the three-deep ranks of men and women we knew well, each waved at us. Judy's eyes were wet with appreciation for the love of the body of Christ for others.

A few days before Christmas I wrapped gifts for our two grandchildren and placed them under the decorated tree. Stepping back for a moment or two I smiled, realizing that the tree itself is nothing more than an ornament to celebrate the reason for the season. That evening the Jacksonville crowd arrived amidst our tears of joy. Once, during the night when one of us got up for a bathroom break, Judy and I had a short conversation about the excitement of having all of the kids and grandchildren at our house for the holiday.

For what would be our final Christmas together Judy said, "No gifts, no card, only a letter," even though we had already given each other a pre-Christmas gift. That way we could tell the family I gave Judy a speaker phone and she gave me an electric razor. I concluded my letter to her with, "Thank you for sharing your life so fully with me, sweetheart. I love you more than life itself, and you will be forever in my heart." My number one job in life was to protect my wife to the best of my ability, not only from external events, but from me as well.

THE HOPE WE HAVE IN CHRIST

Half way between Christmas Day and New Year's Day Judy made a request as she completed her descent from the second floor. "Let's do Chinese!" she said. We immediately went to The China Garden for shrimp fried rice. We had been there many, many times through more than 25 years, but on that day a new waiter noticed our crosses. He commented on the one Judy had recently given me, exclaiming, "That's a Star of David on the face of the cross! Are you Jewish?" I replied, "No, but my Messiah is. Are you a believer?" He smiled broadly and said, "Yes!"

The next evening we were honored to have a Stephen Minister and her three children bring us dinner. Before they left I lifted up her family in prayer. Then the mother shared with us what her 4-year old had asked them during Christmas. "How many Jesuses are there?" he had asked. When told there was only one, he further asked, "How can He be in so many hearts?" Would that adults had the faith of little children.

I had not gone to church in about two months as of January 2005, not wanting to leave Judy, and she not being able to go with me. I was feeling a bit dry in my prayer time, both personally and with her. I went to church service and my heart was refilled. I went home and immediately shared with her what the service had meant to me. The bottom line was that to worry is to distrust God. Worry puts us in the center, instead of God. In fact, when we worry we forget that we can't see the whole picture, which God clearly sees. Worrying quenches the work of God in us and causes us to forget that we were made to revolve around Him, not the other way around. If the purpose of prayer is about getting to know the Father–and I believe it is–then that was the point at which I resolved to more wholeheartedly commune with Him.

Judy and I had another date for lunch. After we had finished eating, one of two ladies sitting in the booth next to us was staring at what I assumed was RAWBi. I was about to comment to her when she said, "I was noticing your cross. It's very unusual."

I thanked her and offered my usual comment on its design, adding that my wife and daughter had it made for me. Then she commented on Judy's cross. At that, Judy proudly showed the woman the teeth marks sunk into the soft gold by our two grandchildren when each of them were babies. It is truly amazing how many times the crosses around our necks were focal points to witnessing to God's glory. When Judy was cremated I honored her request to have her cross placed around her neck. Because she so treasured those particular moments when, as she had held her grand babies, their teeth simply found a purchase on the cross hanging from around her neck. I suspect the reason for her request was one last way of hanging onto her grandchildren, whom she so dearly loved.

LOVE GOD, LOVE PEOPLE

As a Stephen Minister I had the privilege of serving three different care receivers over a three-year period. My second wife, Helga, served for a total of nearly four years, and for more than a year and a half we served together.

Interestingly, Judy and I once ministered to a husband and his ex-wife at the same time. Strangely, both he and his ex-wife came to our house together to bring a meal and break bread with us. Things were actually simpler than they might seem. They had each wanted to help us and so decided to do it together. After the delightful lunch, Judy and my friend's wife ministered to and prayed with one other on the main floor, while my friend and I went to the lower floor to discuss his upcoming surgery and lift that up to the Lord.

Near the end of his and my time together he handed me a slim, black portfolio, saying, "If something goes wrong, give this to my ex." Thanks be to God the operation went well. Moreover, before long he had not only recovered from the surgery, but his prayer life returned, he found re-employment, he cut back on his cigarette smoking, and even found a Christian lady friend. His former wife moved solidly forward on her own way as well.

One week in mid-January Martin picked up Wendi and Abigail at the airport as they had flown in for a visit. A church friend had arranged for our twelve-year old granddaughter to attend middle school student services on Sunday. After their service an older sister of her assigned "buddy" asked about Abigail's church in Jacksonville. Abigail told her they were Gentile members of a Messianic Jewish congregation. The girl then asked what that was. Abigail explained, to which the interested girl's response was, "I thought all Jews were non-believers." Abigail responded with, "Not at all. Jesus was a Jew. And most, if not all, of Jesus' disciples were Jewish." Her new friend said, "Of course, I just never thought of it." When Judy heard the story she said, "Way to go, Abigail!"

One evening Judy said to me, "Well, we're starting our second year of retirement." That reminded me of the list of 55 items on my "to be done" list, compiled shortly after Judy's diagnosis nearly a year earlier. What had I accomplished since then, aside from the single most important job ever entrusted to me: the care of my terminally ill wife? Well, all but ten items had been crossed off my list! Of the ten, four were jobs I would really only need to do if the house were to be sold. I continued to put those off.

When the hospice chaplain came for his appointment one day he made a point of asking us about what we *hadn't* discussed with him, whatever that might be. He said he was glad to see Judy address the possibility of death due to her illness. She then shared with him that her greatest concern was for the family she would be leaving behind. I had much more trouble with that discussion than she did.

What connection can you imagine between egg drop soup and donut holes? As Judy and I and Martin were returning home from church via The China Garden and their delicious egg drop soup, I asked her if she wanted to make another stop for anything. She immediately said, "Donut holes, please." We picked up 25 jelly-filled donut holes and no sooner had we gotten inside the house than she ate three of them. When I challenged her enthusiasm she said, "I would have eaten them in the car if they hadn't been in the back seat!"

I WILL HAVE MERCY ON WHOM I HAVE MERCY

In January of '05 I wrote the following to our newsletter audience on the occasion of Judy's eleventh- month update.

Hallelujah! After nearly a week of Judy's nightly experience of shortness of breath when she required a dose of Morphine to restore relatively free breathing, she has now gone nearly a week without that need. She is an official prayer warrior with our church and prays at length for many others–most of whom she does not know—every day. I was always inspired by Judy's prayerful attitude in that when she wasn't praying for others her prayers were in praise of God.

The Holy Bible clearly tell us that faith alone in Christ alone is the only Way (yes, the Bible is full of absolutes), and that we are saved from His righteous wrath through such faith. Permit me to expand that premise a bit.

When the first man, Adam, chose to disobey God's command, this otherwise-intended immortal and all of his descendants gave rise to everything from disease, war, and suffering to natural catastrophe. While God is the author of individually-perceived calamities, he is not the author of evil, the doorstep of which is crossed through the free will of man. Marvin J. Rosenthal–editor and publisher of *Zion's Fire* magazine puts it this way: "Every broken body, every hurting heart, every disturbed mind–the collective tears of humanity–for at least 6,000 years can trace its origin back to the sin of Adam and Eve in the Garden of Eden."

Now, let us consider what followed that original transgression. As man—at Satan's encouragement—degenerated further and further there came a time when only Noah , his wife, three sons and three daughters-in-law "found grace in the eyes of the Lord" (Genesis 6:8). The universal flood that followed destroyed a wicked humanity, save the eight who would repopulate the earth. As an aside, this was one of two times in man's history that the light of God nearly went out for us, the other being the time of the Tower of Babel when He confused our languages because we felt we could band together and find our own way to the heavens. "Let him who thinks he stands take heed lest he fall" (1 Corinthians 10:12).

With yet more time the fallen angel Satan found a wicked man to foster a counterfeit government and religion in Babylon. But God had accounted Abraham as righteous and covenanted with him that all the nations of the world would be blessed through him (Genesis 12:3).

Through all the above God pointed to our genesis and "the seed of the woman" who, when He (the Savior of mankind) appeared, would be the prophet, priest, and king—that is, the Messiah—who would offer an acceptable sacrifice for man's sin. The unsaving animal sacrifices of the Old Testament had merely pointed the way to the unblemished lamb of the Messianic sacrifice for mankind's sins; past, present and future.

Nearly 800 years after the death of the last of the three Hebrew patriarchs—Abraham, Isaac, and Jacob—God appointed David King of Israel and unconditionally covenanted with him as well. Through Abraham and David's line would come the savior. In fact, the first verse of the first chapter of the New Testament opens with support for this very statement: "The book of the generation of Jesus Christ: the son of David, the son of Abraham" (Matthew 1:1).

What were we made for? To know God. Exactly how much God loved us and the lengths to which He would go to save us from His righteous wrath would prove to be awesome indeed. The Messiah of Israel and the Savior of the world would leave heaven to come to earth in the form of man to bring us God's eternal plan. Jesus the prophet, priest and king would offer us the opportunity for a once-and-for-all sacrifice for sin. Amazingly, He would then turn and make Himself that very sacrifice. As a result, those who simply but clearly accept God's free gift of salvation can say, "It is no longer I who live, but Christ who lives in me." To put it another way, God recognizes our identity by our spiritual birth and not by our behavior.

It was for this gift of Christ in her that Judy has trusted absolutely in Him through her suffering of the past eleven months from cancer's inexorable draining of energy from her body. She yet trusts in Him for this life on earth and her life without end in His presence. She knows, beyond the shadow of a doubt, that not only is God in control, but that His agenda will also be best for her, that she will be both healed and home.

Judy never asked, "Why me, Lord?" And she never complained of her lot. What she did ask was, "What shall I do in reaction to what has befallen me?" Although she may not have fully understood the words in Romans 9:15a, she nevertheless placed her full trust in His Word. For just as God told Moses, He tells us also, 'I will have mercy on whom I have mercy.'"

MAN'S HELL-BENT REBELLION

A simple thought took root in my mind as Judy and I again watched the CD of our all-time favorite musical, *Singing In The Rain*. The passing thought was that should this disease take Judy, I didn't know if I would ever be able to watch this movie again. Well, I was wrong about that because when Helga came into my life months after Judy had been promoted to her heavenly home, I managed to do that very thing, although not without difficulty. God uses both time and faith to help heal the sick.

It was during a late January morning in 2005, during my quiet time, that another, somewhat deeper thought came to me as I was again reading from the book of Job and his great despair which culminated in him questioning God. In paraphrase of the Bible's description of God's reaction to Job, the point for both Job and us is this: "What part of 'Where were you when I laid the foundations of the universe?' don't you get?"

In other words, there is the arrogance of having had some success in life whereby we become more proud of our achievement or status than we are humble for the blessings in and of life. Are we not hell-bent in our rebellion against God's heaven-sent sacrifice? The fact is that of ourselves we can do nothing, but sometimes God has to pry our fingers off of things we *think* we can handle.

As I mentioned earlier, Judy regularly asked the Lord to search her heart and if He should find any little corner where she had some hidden spot of unforgiveness, to reveal that to her so that she could correct it. She loved for me to read the Biblical reference passage for this prayer from Psalm 139:23-24: "Search me, O God, and know my heart; test me and know my anxious thoughts. See if there is any offensive way in me, and lead me in the way everlasting." The NIV Bible commentary refers to this as "exploratory surgery for sin." Interestingly, it wasn't long after that point in time that a member of our MOW group extemporaneously recited from memory, for those of us present, the entire 24 verses of Psalm 139!

GOD'S GRACE

I'm not certain I can properly explain God's grace other than to humbly point to my own life. But for the grace of God I would be lost. By that I mean what happened to me after I fell away from the fringes of interest in God at age 18 and He subsequently let me wander in my unfaithfulness for forty years until age 58, I was yet able to accept His free gift of grace. Simply put, I finally drew the breath that allowed me to draw close to Him, and as a result He then drew close to me.

In 2003 I wrote and had published a Christian science fiction novel in which its theme spoke to the challenge of a truly universal God. The point I tried to make was that if intelligent life does also exist elsewhere in the universe, that life reports to the same God as you and me, for there cannot be competing Creators. God's grace.

Given that we must trust in God—and thus in His Messiah to be saved and have everlasting life—why would God actually bother saving the likes of us from His righteous wrath? The answer lies in Romans 8:32. "He who did not spare even His own Son, but gave Him up on behalf of us all–is it possible that, having given us His Son, He would not give us everything else, too?" God's grace.

I think it's a good question to ask what this verse really means. It means that we are among His creation. That He is the Potter. That we are the clay. That He is our heavenly Father who loves His children, even you and me. Thus, pathetic sinners that we are, is this not the ultimate grace f rom God?

Even more, why would He *also* bother to actually come to earth in the form of a man and live among us, as opposed to His merely instructing us as He did via His prophets from the Old Testament? That, too, is God's incredible grace.

And we can add yet more. Why has God also bothered to carefully explain His eternal plan of salvation that even the least of us can understand? The fact is that He patiently asks exactly how our sins against Him could be atoned if there is no blood sacrifice *we* could make to atone for our sin? How indeed? The answer is simply this: Through Christ's shed blood! And that through God's grace.

Importantly, within the concept of grace I think we must understand this: If the first coming of the Messiah is the most complete revelation of God—and it is—then the simple truth is that we cannot fully know God apart from Christ. And because God appointed Jesus to bring God and man together, we cannot come to God by another path. Hallelujah! That is truly God's grace.

God's greatest gift to us is to allow us to know Him. He is truly only a breath away and each of us draw that breath in our own special way. Judy drew close to Him at age five. As a result, God drew close to her and never left her through her adolescence or through her marriage and motherhood. And it is quite evident that He never left her through her illness. Through all of that He drew even closer to her. She lived to joyfully honor and obey Him, delighting in His ways.

Although I am naturally prejudiced, I believe Judy wonderfully exhibited through most of her life all nine of the fruits of the Spirit as listed in Galatians 5:22-23: love, joy, peace, patience, kindness, goodness, faithfulness, gentleness, and self-control. I can't say the same for myself, as I fall far short with respect to patience, and at times leaving much to desire in the way of self-control. He is with Judy today, and will be with her throughout everlasting life. God's grace.

SPREADING ONE'S JOY

Speaking of joy, one morning, as Judy and I were making our ritual stair descent to the main floor of our house–her hand placed in support on my shoulder—it suddenly came to me to sing a few bars from a popular tune from the 1950's entitled, *I Wonder Why*. I changed only one word–"head" to "hand"—and here is how the lyrics went:

> Put your hand on my shoulder. You need someone who's older.
> A rubdown with a velvet glove!
> There is nothing you can take to relieve this pleasant ache.
> You're not sick, you're just in love."

From then on we had a great deal of fun singing this little ditty together nearly every time we made the trip down the stairs.

In response to my Judy updates/newsletters over many months, we certainly received many encouraging and appreciative notes from friends within the church, but also some from former customers and good friends not connected with our church. One letter came from a self-described agnostic friend. His letter of encouragement prompted me to respond. What follows are excerpts from my subsequent letter to him:

"Dear (Friend), even though you claim to be someone who holds that ultimate causes (such as God) are unknowable, you acknowledge the fact that you not only believe in miracles (whether through divine intervention or other cause), but have been *praying* for us! By virtue of these things and your very significant comment that you are truly searching and assimilating what has been put into your path, it is my contention that you *do* actually believe in a Creator. More evidence lies in the fact that you clearly exhibit a desire to follow your conscience in matters of helping and encouraging others. That is God working in your heart. You are seeking Him.

"When you pray but are not directing that prayer to some particular entity, you are nevertheless praying in order to be heard. There is only one entity who hears prayers, however, and that is God. At the risk of offending you, I have to say that you may as well openly accept His existence—and His Word become flesh—because I have no doubt He is—sooner or later—going to reveal Himself to you in either some subtle or powerful fashion. That is, of course, providing you don't wrap your NSX around a tree before it happens. Thank you for being such a true friend. It is *you* who has blessed us through our friendship. Judy's and my best to you."

Three housecleaning ladies were finishing up their twice-monthly service at our house and they brought Judy a Valentine along with a pretty ceramic vase. They had a substitute worker with them on that particular day and as she was dusting our library shelves in my basement office she said to me, "Do you ever loan any of your books?" I replied, "Of course we do. Which book do you have in mind?"

She said, "Well, I was raised a Baptist but I fell away and stopped going to church. I've been studying other religions and now that I've read *The Da Vinci Code* I really have questions. I need to see some rebuttal."

Wow, what more could an evangelical ask in the way of a witnessing opportunity? I quickly said, "We have just the book for you. First of all you should know that *The Da Vinci Code* is nothing more than an unbeliever's elaborate attempt to make a case for both his unbelief and his bank account. It's a novel, a work of fiction." Since she indicated she was an avid reader I gave her a copy of *The Da Vinci Code Deception*, which focuses on that very subject. By then, Judy had joined us and she gave the seeker a big hug.

Every morning Judy and I thanked God for those whom he would inevitably put in our paths as we would ask for opportunities to witness to His glory. God is most glorified when we are most satisfied in Him. Sometimes, however, one's witnessing efforts can backfire. During Judy's illness, and in the course of my many updates/newsletters, I took a phone call from a family member. Several years earlier my middle brother had passed away after many years of an illness, during all of which my sister-in-law cared for Michael with every bit of love and tenderness possible. Neither of them had an interest in Christian faith, however, of which I was well aware. I, nevertheless, had kept her on my e-mail distribution list. Finally, she said in her e-mail, "I received your latest newsletter, but from now on I only want to know how Judy is doing. You can skip the Jesus stuff."

I called her and overreacted, saying, "I can drop you from my e-mail list, but I won't create another update e-mail for you because this is how I deliver the news." Things got a little frosty and ended on a superficially polite note. I prayed about that exchange for two days before sending her an e-mail apology for my curt, un-Christian response on the telephone. She forgave me and I took her off my newsletter mailing list.

The world cannot tolerate absolutes, but that is God the Creator's nature. It is sad for believers to see anyone–friend or family–reject the God of the universe's teaching, but He has told us plainly we will be rejected for His sake and in fact families will be torn apart because of Him.

Some people think this is harsh, and frankly, so did I in my days of unbelief. I go to my Bible for support on this matter. In Luke 12:51-53 we find some of the hardest teachings of Christ: "Do you think I came to bring peace on earth? No, I tell you, but division. From now on there will be five in one family divided against three. They will be divided against each other, three against two and two against three. They will be divided, father against son and son against father, mother against daughter and daughter against mother, mother-in-law against daughter-in-law and daughter-in-law against mother-in-law."

Why does this have to be? Because Jesus demands a response. There is no middle ground with Jesus. And the bottom line is that for our loved ones (those who are not walking with Christ) to gain everlasting life we must risk our family's approval by taking the message of the gospel to them. Of course, if they simply do not want to hear it, all we can do, sadly, is to respect their request.

In any event, we are not to keep our joy to ourselves. Whether through song, letter, in-person, or any other form, those who rejoice in the Lord must spread that joy in ways they are able. We have to ask ourselves, "How will God use me to challenge the gates of hell?" In other words, how do I make a difference?

SQUIRRELS FLY AND BOOKS SPEAK

Our fenced patio was a veritable small animal-and-bird park. With a bird-and-squirrel feeder complex that included dependable and even interesting food stations for Cardinals, Finches, Hummingbirds, and other flying feeders, as well as both ground and tree squirrels, Judy took great delight in watching our home-grown aviary and critter playground from her family-room perch. One afternoon, shortly after I had just installed an innovative bird feeder with a special weight-sensitive perching bar (which kept both squirrels and larger birds from enjoying the smorgasbord), a young tree squirrel decided to test it for the irresistible seed offerings. As he stepped onto the spinner-perch his weight depressed the battery-operated bar and it slowly began to spin.

The squirrel reacted as if he had simply slipped, clutching the spinner bar even more securely. With his front feet clinging to the bar, his hind legs and feet were suddenly stretched out parallel to the ground as the bar continued to rotate. The bar went around four times with the squirrel comically hanging on as if for dear life. Finally, he had enough and loosed his grip with his front feet, sending him flying into the nearby bush. When he appeared on the ground a few seconds later he bounded to our glass patio door and stood on his hind feet, looking directly at us. Then he began to flap his tail, appearing to scold us (or maybe himself). Judy laughed so hard tears ran down her cheeks and she had to check herself.

With that diversion to see me off, I drove into midtown Atlanta to a vintage book store I had phoned the day before. I had inquired as to their interest in three first edition books by London, Sartre, and Steinbeck, which I had inherited from my middle brother. I hadn't discussed specifics with the store's owner but I thought two of them might be worth $100-$200 each, and maybe more for the Steinbeck first American edition of *The Grapes of Wrath*.

As it turned out they were interested all right, to the point of offering me a total of $25 for all three books. Worse, I took the deal! Even worse than that, my car wouldn't start when I went to leave, leaving me to have the car towed to a nearby garage. They couldn't fix my car until the next day so I called a taxi for the 25-mile ride home.

Now it would seem that I did not have a profitable day in the offing, and you may also be wondering how this might even vaguely fit with our testimony. Let's see what I can do with that. On the way home I called Judy to bring her up to date. She didn't think I should have sold the books at all, but she got a good laugh out of my having negotiated such a "fine" deal.

The mid-forties taxi driver wasn't very chatty considering he had a good fare on board. He had overheard me talking to Judy, however, and when I hung up he said, "I've read one of those books, Sartre's *The Age of Reason*." To that he added, "He was a good writer, but I don't think much of the French these days. They're short on memory when it comes to war."

Surprised, but finding his comment interesting, I pondered as we rode for a little longer. Then I proceeded to tell him I had written three books myself, two of which were Christian novels. I followed that with the question, "Do you know Jesus?"

He answered simply, "No." I responded with, "You ought to get to know our Lord and Savior, George. I didn't come to know Him until I was 58 years old and it turned my life around." He made no comment.

We rode a little farther in silence so I turned to prayer, asking God to give me the words to witness since we had a 40-minute ride ahead of us. Following that I reasoned that since I was the buyer in this transaction I could reasonably pursue my witness. I asked him if he had ever played golf. He gave me another two-letter answer. I persisted, saying, "That's the background of one of my novels; a foursome playing a round of golf and involving lots of verbal fireworks concerning faith or no faith in Christ." He offered zip for comment.

I persisted. "The foursome's make-up is that of an atheist, an agnostic, a Jewish religious skeptic and a born-again Christian," I said, hoping he might place himself in one of the categories and by so doing lead to some discussion. Nothing. I tried once more. "Before I began writing the story, George, I hadn't even known what a born-again Christian was. That's because I had no definable faith myself." Still nothing.

I was down but not out. I told him that in doing research for writing the novel I had read the Bible from cover to cover and in that process came to accept Jesus Christ as my Lord and Savior. That didn't move him either. Finally, in desperation, I said, "George, when we get to my house I'll give you a copy of my book, if you'll read it."

Surprise! He said, "Okay I might read it. But tell me, how did you know my name? It isn't printed anywhere in the car." I had to laugh out loud. I obviously hadn't gotten to him with my witness, but I had finally gotten a reaction. Who am I to question how the Lord uses us to get someone's attention? I told him the name thing was a fluke. I had seen his small "I'm a Georgia voter" sticker on the dashboard but it had curled with the sun's heat of the day and the copy was rumpled. I assumed it might be a name badge reading 'George.'

He absorbed my explanation but said nothing. In the inside rear view mirror, however, I could see him smiling. When we got to my house I went inside to get him a copy of the book in which I wrote, "Thanks for the ride, George. May God continue to bless you." I gave him the book and paid him, along with a generous tip. He accepted both and looked at me with a perplexed expression which I couldn't grasp. I do think, however, that I did all God asked of me in that circumstance. When I regaled Judy with the rest of my odyssey she said it made her day.

The point of it all? We are told to be prepared to explain the hope one has in Christ.

HOLY CABINET AND PAPER CUPS

Her cancer could not keep Judy down. Even into her final months I would run an errand and return home to find her doing some non-strenuous household chore, or at least trying. The cleaning chore she most regularly wanted done, of course, was the washing and drying of clothes. For years I used to brag to my bachelor racquetball buddies about having a mysterious cabinet built into a bedroom wall in our home.

How did it work? It accepted my dirty clothes, but then something happened to them that within a few days the clothes were miraculously returned–cleaned and folded, even ironed if needed–to my dresser drawer and closet! I told them that since they didn't like doing that sort of home labor they should go to Home Depot and buy one of these "holy" cabinets. That is, if they hadn't sold out. They never seemed to even marginally appreciate the humor. That didn't keep me from frequently using it, however.

For months Judy had been using hand towels which I would pin under her chin to both sides of her night sweater. These were for the purpose of absorbing the sputum she involuntarily gave up while sleeping. She had suddenly begun soaking as many as three towels a night, necessitating my changing them as often. She once soaked a record eighteen towels in a single night.

One morning, Judy and I found ourselves confronted by a rare circumstance. We had a mildly argumentative discussion about her not wanting to go to church. That also meant I couldn't go because

I could not leave her. I felt she was overreacting to the potential for catching a cold from being in a crowded sanctuary, which she felt–given her lowered immunity—could quickly escalate into something serious. I told her we could sit in either the sparsely occupied balcony or in a crying room. Neither of us could seem to see the other's point. After about an hour of mutual pouting we decided to pray about it and leave things there. Even though we did not go to bed that night upset with one another, this serves as an example of my having to work at protecting her from myself.

The next day we were distracted by other matters. We received the good news that our application for Medicare's Assistance Program had been approved for a significant patient assistance amount, good against either future co-payment cancer prescription drugs or retroactive use. Wow! That meant the money that had been spent the year before for a three-month supply of the IRESSA drug–an incredible expense neither Medicare nor our secondary insurance paid for—would be coming back to us. Kevin and Wendi had actually paid about two-thirds of the tab while we covered the other third. I e-mailed the kids the good news but they declined repayment for their part, saying it would be "too difficult a bookkeeping chore." Yeah, right. Judy's reaction was, "Thank you, kids. Thank you, Lord."

Some years earlier Judy had worked for Kimberly-Clark as an administrative assistant and she commented that we should buy some of her former employer's stock. I asked her what she meant by that. She said, "On account of all the paper cups I use!" I took a few minutes to calculate a bit of trivia and opined that in the previous twelve month period she had used more than 6,000 9-oz. paper cups in coughing up water from her lungs. I still wasn't moved to buy any K-C stock.

REJOICING THROUGH ONE'S TRIALS

Judy was such an inspiration to me. Even though she suffered in her weakened condition she never worried (insulted God) nor complained (judged God). Rather, she both took joy and rejoiced in God's will. Do you know what Scripture tells us about faith in that respect? It says that faith is authentic when it rejoices in trials. Wow! Now, don't misunderstand. I don't mean Judy actually rejoiced in *having* her trials, rather, she rejoiced *through* them. That is, she asked God's wisdom to endure them, for in the endurance of one's trials, perseverance is produced (James 1:2-6). This prompts another reality. We can't truly know the depth of our character until we see how we react under pressure.

At about this time in caring for Judy I had a fascinating dream. It was almost certainly stimulated by something I had read earlier that same day. What I had read, my actual dream, and their underlying message dealt with the notion that by judging others we must also realize the discomfort of being judged.

I dreamt I was sitting on a bench surrounded by an ethereal mist. I was not alone, however, for the infinitely linear bench was filled with countless other people. I don't recall how we were dressed but we were all simply waiting. One-by-one the person at the head of the bench was somehow summoned through a nondescript door.

After a surprisingly short wait there was only one person ahead of me. To him I spoke for the first time, saying, "Do you think we're being summoned for judgement for the things we did or did not do in life?"

The other fellow responded with a sniff of satisfaction and said, "I hope so. I admit that I didn't expect anything of this sort, but I think the scales of justice will balance out in my favor." To that, the fellow sitting directly behind me on the bench, said, "I wish I could be so certain of that. On the one hand I have never committed any serious sins, but on the other hand I have rarely missed attending church. Nevertheless, I am afraid." Then he asked me a question: "How are you going to plead?"

"Guilty," I said.

He was surprised by my plea and said with a fearful look in his eyes, "But won't that be your ticket to hell?"

I replied, "If you mean hell is what I deserve, then the answer is 'yes.' But I'm trusting in my attorney to get me off."

"Attorney?" he said, incredulous at the comment. "How do you know you'll be allowed a defense?"

I answered with one word, "Romans."

"Romans?" he responded. "Your attorney is a soldier?"

"No," I said, shaking my head. "Romans 8:32 of the Holy Bible. 'He who did not spare even His own Son, but gave Him up on behalf of us all—is it possible that, having given us His Son, he would not give us everything else, too?'"

"The fellow shook his head and said, "I don't understand."

I tried to explain, saying, "What you or I or anyone at judgment time will not find beneficial is to present a list of good deeds."

"Why not?" he persisted.

"Because," I said, "the judge will then ask us about our ten thousand sins of both commission and omission."

"Well," the fellow said sarcastically, "your defense attorney must be in the 'know' if he can get you off after a guilty plea."

I said, "He certainly is. And as a matter of fact, He could do the same for both you and the fellow in front of us."

"And how is that?" he said, more skeptical than hopeful, it seemed to me.

I was, nevertheless, encouraged and so continued. "By your faith in His ability to defend you. In fact, my attorney always lives to intercede for those whose names are written in the Book of Life."

"I don't like how this is going," he said, and added, "But what about an appeal?"

Then I felt I had to get into his face a little, and so made my argument. "Brother, we all have a lifetime for appeal. Human beings are appointed to die once, but after that comes judgment. Once life passes it is too late. Our fate is fairly determined by the way we respond to the Gospel preached to us."

The other fellow tried to brush off my obviously disturbing comments with attempted humor, saying, "Is your attorney Jewish by chance?"

"Not by chance," I said, "but yes. He is the Jewish Messiah, Christ Jesus. He is the One who will mediate the case of all believers to the Father."

Then the fellow stated the obvious, saying, "I was afraid of that. I am undone, for I have no relationship with Him."

End of story. My apologies to whoever penned the original, but sketchy metaphoric dialogue, with which I have taken significant literary liberties.

My Sunday School teacher often comments about God's healing with respect to *unbelievers*: The point is that those who do not know the Lord may be healed by medicine–and possibly by miracles (just as with believers)–but they may *not* be healed through Christ's resurrection, because they will not be in God's presence (Truth) and thus cannot be made perfect through Christ's sacrifice for those who believe. Why is that so? Quite simply, it is because God's holiness will not allow for our unholy nature to exist in His holy presence.

When Judy died she was glorified before God because of her faith. She was justified in Him. In other words, she could have said it was *just as if I had* not sinned. Just-if-i-ed.

If you, dear reader, have somehow plodded through the book to this point and do not truly have a personal (that is, a praying) relationship with Jesus Christ, you may well say to yourself, "Why don't all these so-called born-again people keep their beliefs to themselves?"

For one, we have no choice but to proclaim the Gospel, for believers are required to make Christ known to all they meet, however they are able. It is also true that each individual must decide for him or herself the life-changing Gospel message. That message changed my life in late middle age, just as surely as God took hold of Judy as a young child and she subsequently learned to commit every situation to God, and trust Him for the outcome. She continued her growth in sanctification to the very end when she was called home and glorified in Him.

In closing this subhead of the book I remind myself that while we all hope for many more days, our focus here and now must be our relationship with Him. So, first comes our relationship, based in trust, and then our works follow. Why in that order? Because we can never sit in judgment of ourselves.

THE POWER OF PRAYER

After sending out my update letter of February '05 I received one very interesting response in which the writer–a former senior pastor of our church–thanked Judy and me for continuing to name the name of Jesus in our lives and ministry. He added that when faced with other options the followers of Jesus have always responded, "Lord, to whom shall we go? You have the words of eternal life." To what was he referring? There is only one God, one Creator. To whom else would we pray?

When James—the brother of Jesus and a believing Jewish leader in the first century Messianic community—wrote a letter to the audience of his day and to all believers everywhere, he devoted a part of what would become the Book of James to the prayer of faith. In 5:16b he took particular pains to speak of the power of prayer in a sentence widely known and quoted to this day: "The prayer of a righteous man is powerful and effective." This statement is hardly a simple cliche, but is an essential part of James' God-breathed work on how-to living for believers in our almighty and everlasting God.

James refers to the prophet Elijah for support in this matter in the succeeding verses. "Now, Elijah was a man just like us. He prayed earnestly that it would not rain and it did not rain on the land for three and a half years. Again, he prayed and the heavens gave rain, and the earth produced its crops."

This was not the only time Elijah prayed and received a powerful response from God. In chapter 18 of the 1 Kings account of Elijah on Mount Carmel, in a confrontation with Ahab concerning the Israelites having abandoned the Lord's commands, there is an even more dramatic example. In the ultimate contest with the 850 prophets brought by Ahab, who, along with his wife–the infamous Jezebel–all worshiped the most popular Canaanite god, Baal, a most remarkable example of the power of prayer occurred. Elijah appealed to the people to choose between Baal and the Lord as to who was God of all. To that end they procured two bulls and cut them into pieces before placing them on two different altars of firewood, but did not set fire to either.

Read the account as written in the Word: Elijah said "Call on the name of your god, and I will call on the name of the Lord. The god who answers by fire–he is God. Then they called on the name of Baal from morning til noon. 'O, Baal, answer us!' they shouted. But there was no response; no one answered. And they danced around the altar they had made.

"At noon Elijah began to taunt them. 'Shout louder! he said. 'Surely he is sleeping and must be awakened.' So they shouted louder and slashed themselves with swords and spears, as was their custom, until their blood flowed. Midday passed, and they continued their frantic prophesying until the time for the evening sacrifice. But there was no response, no one answered, no one paid attention.

"Then Elijah said to all the people, 'Come here to me.' They came to him, and he repaired the altar of the Lord, which was in ruins. Elijah took twelve stones, one for each of the tribes descended from Jacob, to whom the word of the Lord had come, saying, 'Your name shall be Israel!' With the stones he built an altar in the name of the Lord, and he dug a trench around it large enough to hold two seahs (about thirteen quarts) of seed.

"He arranged the wood, cut the bull into two pieces and laid it on the wood. Then he said to them, 'Fill four large jars with water and pour it on the offering and on the wood. Do it again,' he said, and they did it again. 'Do it a third time,' he ordered, and they did it the third time. The water ran down around the altar and even filled the trench.

"At the time of the sacrifice, the prophet Elijah stepped forward and prayed, 'O Lord, God of Abraham, Isaac, and Israel (Jacob), let it be known today that you are God in Israel and that I am your servant and have done all these things at your command. Answer me, O Lord, so that these people will know you, O Lord, are God, and that you are turning their hearts back again.

"Then the fire of the Lord fell and burned up the sacrifice, the wood, the stones and the soil, and also licked up the water in the trench. When all the people saw this, they fell prostrate and cried, 'The Lord–he is God! The Lord—he is God!'"

Faith. We walk by faith and not by sight. My point is this: Prayer is not only powerful . . . and every single believer has prayer available to him . . . but the God of the universe created us with that very thing in mind: that we would commune with Him about any–and every—thing.

BELIEVE-IT-OR-NOT

During Judy's illness she and I together viewed a CD of *The Jesus Film* in our home. She was quite moved by it. If you are not familiar with this it is one of the most accurate films ever produced on the life of Christ. The film is a project of a ministry of Campus Crusade for Christ International and they refer to the film as being "the very Word of God," since every word spoken by the actor portraying Jesus is a direct quote from scripture.

I received an incredible printed testimony from The Jesus Film Project people in Orlando, Florida and it was so exceptional I wanted to include it here (with express permission) as another powerful witness for prayer.

An evangelist was leading a *Jesus* team into difficult regions of Africa, taking the film to people who had never heard the Gospel's message. This particular team was headed for a large village and had sent a co-worker ahead to arrange a meeting with the chief to ask his permission to show the *Jesus* film.

The worker tried fruitlessly to persuade the chief but he wanted nothing to do with "*Jesus*" and declared, "I am a Muslim, I am a Muslim leader. I lead the mosque and I'm chief of the village. Since this village has existed we have never allowed any other religion. You will do *nothing* here!"

The team leader, who then arrived in support of his worker, respectfully replied, with the Holy Spirit as his guide, "We are coming here to show you and your people the *Jesus* film, preach the gospel and heal the sick." The chief responded with, "What did you say? Heal the sick? . . . Really? . . . Is that possible?"

The team leader said, "Yes, if you allow us to show the *Jesus* film and preach the gospel." The chief looked at his second-in-command and fell silent. There was a pause as he thought. Finally, the chief turned to the team leader and said, once again, "Really? Heal the sick? Okay. We want to see this." With his permission the team went to work in a large soccer field. They unloaded the projection equipment and generator, and threaded the film, set up the screen, speaker and lights. Then, they went about announcing the film.

Around 5,000 people came that night and filled the soccer field. It was S.R.O. and something was obviously happening. As the film began the team leader went to his vehicle and prayed, asking God to give him a word for those people once the film had concluded.

The people were deeply moved as they watched and listened to the words in their own language. So much was literally foreign to them, yet so wondrous. They were stunned by the life of this good Man, His crucifixion, and resurrection. The team leader said that people were listening in a way he had never seen in all the many outreaches in which he had participated. He said he felt like the Holy Spirit was hovering over the entire soccer field and village, "calling them out of darkness."

Over the microphone he then called out, "How many here recognize a need for a Savior?" Almost everyone raised his hand. There was a group of young people on his right. Some raised their hands and voices, "We want our sins to be forgiven!" Then others on the other side of the team leader cried out, "We want our sins to be forgiven!"

Then everyone began crying out to God for mercy. In that moment, the leader led the entire group of 5,000 in the prayer of salvation. Then he spoke to the crowd, saying, "This Jesus is not only a Savior, but He is a Healer, and today He wants to heal anybody who is sick. Bring your sick forward." So, one by one, they came–first, about twelve men and women with back problems. With the power of the Holy Spirit he healed them all, instantly. Then, seeing this, they brought a young deaf boy, about eight years old. The Lord healed him. People kept coming, and kept being healed. God was obviously at work affirming His Word and His Son! The team leader uses the ever-so-common word, *incredible*, in its ultimate application.

On the leader's right stood the chief, the leader of the village and the mosque. Turning to him the leader said, "Do you see what is happening?" The chief answered, "Yes. Can I say something to my people?" The leader gave him the microphone and stepped aside. To the 5,000 the chief said, "What you have just seen is real because there is no man who can do what you have seen unless God is with him, and these people who have come to us. The Lord is with them. Now, bring all the sick from the village! Go home, now, and bring them here!"

Wow, a story from 2006 happening just as we might expect from the pages of scripture. This witness is certainly a wonderful lesson, and I do not for one moment believe it was meant for nothing, for God's word never returns void. Neither does the faith and trust we place in Him.

PUTTING ON A HAPPY FACE

A few minutes before Judy and I were about to depart for our 46th wedding anniversary luncheon (the last one we would share), a highly unusual avian event took place on our patio. For several years our back yard had been regularly visited by a Red Tailed Hawk, but the closest we had ever seen it was high in a tree ten yards from the back of the house. As Judy watched from her chair in the family room I was finishing the folding of the last of a washer load of clothes.

I sat on the family couch a few feet from the glass patio door (the same door through which the squirrel had scolded us a few weeks earlier). As I flopped a folded white T-shirt onto the stack of clothes in front of me our huge occasional Hawk resident suddenly swooped down from his perch on a low-hanging branch only a few yards from the patio door. He struck the glass—talons forward–and bounced off. Surprisingly, he appeared to lose neither his balance nor his composure as he shook his feathers before flapping off.

We surmised that this hunter-bird had mistaken the flopping piece of linen for prey. Judy and I witnessed the entire scenario and marveled at having been allowed to see such a happening in nature. For months following that event Judy would comment to the stream of family and visitor well-wishers, "This patio is my world of entertainment, from Hummingbirds and Cardinals to squirrels and Hawks."

A few days later I heard Judy's voice on the intercom, softly repeating my name. I dashed up two flights of stairs from my office to check on her. In obvious pain, she said slowly, "I think I need the medicine." I knew she meant Morphine. I gave her three drops and waited ten minutes, but the pain of her TN/sinus had not let up. I gave her another three drops and began preparing some hot tea for her. In between the two medications she had said, "I can usually put on a happy face for others, but I can be honest with you. If it weren't for this terrible sinus pain I would be fine." That was courageous, but not accurate, for the cancer was killing her.

We can tell, teach, or write what we believe, but we can only reproduce who we are. We must, therefore, be good models. For me, that statement–at the time—meant two things. One, Judy was the model. Two, her model begged ever more urgently my need for God's grace.

That Easter Sunday of 2005 I typed my day's journal notes through tears. Judy had been in nearly constant pain from her TN/sinus condition for four consecutive days. She could not chew food without pain. She could not talk normally without pain. Even hard-sound consonants caused her pain in their pronunciation. She could not even sleep without bearing pain.

In spite of that we gathered ourselves and thanked the Lord for our plenty. Family joined us in the afternoon. Judy positively reveled in having family around and would not miss it even in her greatest moments of pain. I do not believe I possess a fraction of her will to function in the face of pain.

KWAK had come to town again for a few days over Easter, and on Monday Kevin and I had some time to ourselves. We talked about Judy. He called the hospice nurse to satisfy himself that their program was up to the task as things might develop. He came away convinced that they were, and that, if and when Judy could not adequately get her breath, that they could come immediately and stay with her for up to 24 hours if necessary. In the worst case scenario, they would admit her to their in-patient hospice unit, which meant I would not have to call 911 and have her futilely treated at the hospital.

Kevin said he was amazed that she was still with us more than a year after the diagnosis; that, given her difficulties, even before Thanksgiving he had told Wendi her mother might not make it to the holiday. He reiterated that same possibility prior to Christmas, but there she was at the end of March, still radiant and fighting. "She is one tough lady," he had said.

As Judy and I drove the four of them to the airport the next day, six-year-old Karsten hugged Judy and said, "I love you forever, Grandma." As the two of us drove home via the "scenic" route we marveled, not only for what God had done through the incredible blessings ("blessing" literally meaning "happy many times over"), but for His awesomeness as the Creator. We were both at peace with things—even though we didn't necessarily understand—simply because we had such faith in Him and in the promise we had through Christ Jesus for everlasting life.

During this difficult time for Judy, our son, Martin and Betty were dealing with her grandmother's failing health. Between the two of them they had made two 1,300 mile round trip drives to Miami to see to see her beloved Ya Ya. Judy was much relieved when they were both safely home to stay, even though the grandmother did pass before long.

A HARD LESSON

At the thirteen-month mark following her diagnosis Judy continued to persevere in the face of her devastating affliction. As everyone knows, cancer wears so many different faces and affects so many people's lives worldwide. Every week in her prayer warrior ministry she would receive a significant number of e-mailed prayer requests, often for those dealing with one or another of cancer's demons. As Judy liked to put it, "God does not give anyone cancer, but He *can* cure." In a note from my beloved late-eighties aunt and uncle in Missouri, my aunt encouraged us, with my uncle adding, "Judy, I'm giving you a direct order. Get well right now, if it be God's will!"

Speaking of God's will, we come to the "difficult Gospel lesson" of my sub-head. Was Jesus' first coming for the purpose of bringing peace on earth? I briefly mentioned this subject lesson earlier in the book. Testifying as to the absolutes about the existence of God and His instructions to us for gaining salvation and thus eternal life are obviously worthy of much repetition. Jesus's first coming was, in fact, for that purpose alone. He answered His own question on the subject of whether or not He had come to bring peace on earth by saying, "No, I tell you, but division."

To this some might say, "Why would the Savior of the World create the potential for such disharmony?" He is saying that choosing to follow Him is not a matter of choosing Christ from among a number of equivalent paths. And because of that statement the road immediately begins to fork. The world cannot tolerate absolutes.

But God not only tells us the very opposite, he says it repeatedly and in no uncertain terms through His prophets, through His apostles, and through His Word made flesh in the form of Jesus Christ. To begin Christ's ministry here on earth a voice from heaven said the moment Jesus came up from the water after His baptism in the Jordan River by John the Baptist, "This is my Son, whom I love; with him I am well pleased" (Matthew 3:17). Consider this absolute, revealed by Jesus as He was instructing His disciples: "No one comes to the Father except through Me" (John 14:6b). Is there any ambiguity there?

As to his authority, Jesus answered His doubters with the clearest statement of His divinity ever made. He was addressing unbelieving Jews in the temple at a time when they were celebrating the Feast of the Dedication (Hanukkah) and was pointedly asked this question: "If you are the Messiah, tell us plainly." To this He responded, "I did tell you, but you do not believe. I and the Father are one" (John 10:25, 30). *I and the Father are one.*

Judy's condition had continued to deteriorate, yet her only comment for the latest update/newsletter was, "I am managing. My quality of life is fine. I'm still here. I trust in Him." Why is the implied faith of such an attitude so important? As one author puts it, "Had death not had the rug pulled right out from under its feet and was subsequently powerless to keep Him in the grave . . . believers in Him would be the sorriest people who ever trod the earth."

HOME AND HEART

Although Judy and I gradually lost the option to take even short walks together, to travel by either car or plane, or even to receive much company, we continued to take great joy from life. We found realtime refuge in Him and counted on the great hope of Scripture's promise to come. You, dear reader, no doubt have serious challenges in life as well, and you can take equally great heart in the hope of His promise to all who believe on Him.

Once, very early in the morning, I was awakened by a strange sound. It was as if Judy's oxygen line wasn't feeding properly. I looked over at her and didn't see the line strung behind her ears or even connected to her nose. What had happened? The oxygen line had gotten tangled up in her bed clothes. There was no determining how long it had been off. Sometimes, when she needed to clean her nosepiece during the night she would fall asleep during the process. As I finished replacing the line I sat opposite her on the footstool holding one of her hands, silently crying as I softly murmured, "Oh, sweetheart, my heart hurts so much for you."

The next day she was hopeful of going out for a pizza lunch but decided against it. Instead, we watched a very interesting public television documentary about the life of black writer Ralph Ellison, author of *The Invisible Man*. I have a reason for mentioning this. The book was published in 1952 and was widely acclaimed as the first significant black novel, but the relevant point comes in the form of a three-word sentence in the story: "Novels can educate."

It came to me that this is exactly what I had tried to do with each of the three novels I had written. I wondered if I would be able to do the same with a testimonial from the voluminous notes I had thus far journaled through Judy's illness.

Between the start of my Stephen Ministry training in early January of 2004 and the time of Judy's passing in September of 2005 I, too, finally understood the apostle Paul's admonition about accepting whatever circumstances in which a person finds himself. I truly became humbled—yet have by no means learned the lesson as well as Judy, for she was ever a courageous and joyful victor.

Through the Stephen Ministry experience I came to much more fully realize that living the Holy life is not attained merely through an affinity for prayer and Bible study. As critical as those are, living the Holy life revolves around God in *every* place at *every* moment. God convicts us, little by little. I earlier made the example of how, immediately upon accepting Christ as my Lord and Savior, I quit using foul language on the racquetball court. Before long a bad back took me out of that game altogether.

A few years later, the Lord called me away from active participation with my lifelong love of golf. I was beginning to understood that as I had come to Him late in life and much more of my life lay behind me than before me, I no longer had five-hour chunks of time for indulging myself in such a fashion. Understand that what I'm saying is a personal thing and is not meant to imply golf is anything but a wonderful recreational activity. I still enthusiastically watch pro golf tournaments on TV.

One afternoon Judy called me in from pitching horseshoes, saying, "You just received a call from the wife of an old family friend in Arizona. Why don't you call her?" Evalyn had left a recorded message and I returned her call. What a story she had to tell.

She related that a week earlier she had felt quite ill and her husband, Paul—age 92 and a staunch believer—was also feeling poorly. Nevertheless, he drove her to the hospital. En route, he became seriously ill. When they arrived at the emergency department she told the admitting people that her husband needed to be seen immediately. Once into the exam room he quickly flat-lined. Those in attendance feverishly worked on him and were apparently able to bring him back. I put it that way because he regained but a moment of life. As he did, his words to his wife were not only clear but instructional as he turned his head to her and said, "Evalyn, you're a widow. Go to the Senior Center."

It is my personal opinion that his strong will and need for closure were such that–in combination with his strong faith—he was somehow allowed an unusual perquisite at the end of his life.

During another evening I turned on the television set to the Music Channel and the Big Band & Swing format. A beautiful, slow tune with a familiar 1940's beat began playing and my thoughts drifted. I asked Judy if she would like to dance. She would and we did, right there in our kitchen. As I held her close, knowing full well it might be the last time we would ever dance together, she knew my eyes were filling with tears. She said to me several times, "It'll be all right." At the moment I was weeping out of sadness. As I type these words tears form anew, but this time it is as much in joy, both for the wonderful memories and for her healing.

A wise person once said, "No winter lasts forever; no spring skips its turn." For those of us who have lost a loved one, it seems at first that death is only an ending. But for the survivor–and this applies as much for divorce as it does death—it must also be a beginning. This is not a beginning most of us ever planned to make and we are poorly prepared. Yet the path to opening our hearts and our minds to accept devastating loss puts us on the path of eventual understanding and healing.

Even more importantly to understand is that this is a path we alone can make meaningful. It is the process of grieving that changes us and finally permits us to emerge from widowhood (or other of life's toughest lessons) to personhood. The transition cannot be rushed, but if we let it, it will happen. Like the spring at the end of a cold and bitter winter, it will come.

DEATH IS NOT THE END OF LIFE

What in our lives deserves broader consideration than life on the other side of death? The most common view of the Church has been that, at death, the soul immediately goes to be with God and there is a continuity of personal existence. In other words, there is no interruption of life at the end of this life. In yet other words, upon death we continue to be alive in our personal souls.

We have persistent examples in Scripture of this notion of continuity. In the Old Testament the bosom of Abraham was seen as the place of the after-life. The apostle Paul put it this way: "To live in this world is good; the greatest thing than can ever happen is to be participating in the final resurrection. But the intermediate state (heaven) is even better." Remember, heaven is not the end either, for resurrection follows that.

In heaven God wipes away the tears from people's eyes for the last time. But is everybody's cup full in heaven? Yes, for we are told that in heaven God's people have become sanctified, justice has been brought to bear, and people have been vindicated. No death, no sorrow, no sickness, no hatred, and no evil. And although many theologians agree that not everybody in heaven has the same size cup (each cup nevertheless being filled), I firmly believe that this is not nearly as important as either getting there or not getting there at all.

The bottom line is simply this: Anyone who is desirous of spending everlasting life in the presence of God–at whatever the capacity of his or her cup–needs to be born again, here and now.

If we were to die without being born again, however, we *would* be dead. How is that, you ask? Well, our sins convict us and we cannot pay the price for them. Jesus Christ, however, was the unblemished lamb (sinless) and he went to the cross and paid the price for our sins, thus defeating death on our behalf. And He did it for one purpose only, so that you and I–those of us who believe in Him–might have everlasting life in Him. Of all the verses in the Bible, no verse promises more than what we read in John 11:25-26, as Jesus Himself said, "I am the resurrection and the life. He who believes in me will live, *even though he dies* (emphasis added); and whoever lives and believes in me will never die."

He who *is* life can surely restore life. Whoever believes in Christ has a spiritual life that lives beyond physical death. But what does it take to cross over from having no future to having a guarantee of the most magnificent future possible . . . eternally? Let me use Judy's passing as an example. Accepting the above truth as she did she could easily have phrased that trust with these words: "Do not weep. I know my Savior."

All any one must do is call on Christ and claim Him as our Savior and Lord. Remember what Jesus said to the thief on the cross after he asked to be remembered: "I say to you, today you shall be with me in paradise." He did not say as much, however, to the other thief on the cross who did *not* ask to be remembered.

I waited 58 years before I responded to His grace and goodness. It is also true that I had absolutely no assurance I might not have passed away on the very eve of the day *before* I finally accepted God's free gift of salvation. Had I gone to the grave with no intention of accepting that gift, I would not have ascended into God's presence for everlasting life. There is no second chance to do so beyond the grave.

CHRIST'S FIRST COMING MERELY "INTERESTING?"

One night I inadvertently interrupted Judy as she was concluding her regular evening's half-hour prayer time for the many on her prayer warrior list. I was apologetic when I realized what I had done, but she said, "You didn't disturb me. You're just in time to help me finish with the Lord's prayer." The next day the word "disturb" was heavy on my mind and that caused me to reflect on something else. When Christ declares Himself to be the Way, the Truth, and the Light, do we fully understand He did not mean that to be merely "interesting" to us? You will shortly see the connection to the word "disturb."

Consider the following core truths in which evangelicals the world over believe:

* ... that the Bible is the inspired, the only infallible and authoritative Word of God
* ... that there is one God, eternally existent in three persons: Father, Son and Holy Spirit
* ... in the deity of our Lord Jesus Christ, in His virgin birth, in His sinless life, in His miracles, in His vicarious and atoning death through His shed blood, in His bodily resurrection, in His ascension to the right hand of the Father, and in His personal return to power and glory.

But there is one more little item for which evangelicals would put their life on the line. That is the belief in the resurrection of both the saved and the lost; they that are *saved* unto the resurrection of life and they that are *lost* unto the resurrection of damnation. We're talking heaven and hell.

As evangelicals, we believe this because the Word of God tells us it is so. Now, I know this last statement about salvation and damnation disturbs–rather than merely "interests"—a lot of people. But consider this: No one can deny that all of us are afflicted with brevity of life, whether that be 50 or 100 years, yet God didn't create man merely to be born, mature (hopefully), and die. Rather, His created beings were brought to life in order to come to worship the Creator for the everlasting life He has promised us.

How sad that so many are willing to settle for the relative happiness (or unhappiness, which is every individual's choice) of this brief life and thus give up everlasting life in absolute joy, merely because of the sins of pride and stubbornness.

The age-old defense of "I've led a good life" (implying that one will be judged righteous and therefore saved from God's wrath) is a totally unfounded opinion without Scriptural authority. Not only has God never said that your (or my) supposed conscientiously led life is good enough, He has unequivocally stated through His Word that no one is righteous. No , not one, neither you nor me. And that's why He saw the need to come to earth in the form of man. He knew we wouldn't get it unless He made His point in person. He also knew only a relative few would get it even then! For more than half a century I was one of those willing to settle for the plodding non-belief of nominal–or lukewarm—Christianity. In such an attitude Jesus did not offer any hope. In fact, he said a person would be as well off in unbelief. Lost is as lost does.

One of the things that has come to disturb me most with respect to trying to carry the message of the Gospel to others is that of an unrepentant person's bold opposition to the very doctrines that provide him with the necessary understanding to know and love God as He has revealed Himself to us. One could arguably say the entire interval between the first and second coming of Christ are "the last days." Therefore, we could argue that you and I live in the very same "last days" as the disciples. My point is that how could anything thus be more urgent than the matter of His return, which could come at literally any moment?

During most of 2004 and 2005 and the days of sharp personal focus on my beloved late wife's life-limiting illness both of us found ourselves joyfully buoyed by our Lord God's promise of eternal salvation through Him. I also know that many might ask, "Can you truly rely on that?"

Hear Jesus' own words relative to this question: "If it were not so I would have told you." But don't misunderstand my joy in His promise for my sadness at Judy's illness. Both of us accepted the circumstances. Judy essentially lived with her cancer in this fashion: "God, I know you can heal me from this cancer, but if You don't I yet trust You in all things, even if I die." Does that have a familiar ring with respect to the answer Shadrach, Meshach, and Abednego gave King Nebuchadnezzar when he threatened them in the fiery funace?

A cardiologist once said this to me about Judy's condition: "People with a slow-growing cancer such as hers suffer less pain than those with a fast-growing cancer." That fact was indeed a blessing of which we were keenly aware. It was ironic that her most intense and persistent pain came not from the cancer itself, but from the sinusitis, yet she always said of that particular affliction, "It is God's mercy that only one side of my face is affected."

ATTITUDE ITSELF A WITNESS

Shortly after I sent out my 14-month Judy update/newsletter I received a responsive e-mail from a good friend I had not necessarily known to be a believer. An excerpt from his letter read, "I really can't tell you the strength I draw from Judy's faith and her spirit in this fight. I appreciate her more than I can communicate in a mere e-mail. I have held off calling you as my emotions continue to overwhelm me any time I let them, so speaking about my faith can be very difficult."

One afternoon I asked Judy if she wanted to go with me to pick up some pizza for dinner. She did, and she waited in the car for me as we had arrived before the pizza was quite ready. I knew it wouldn't be unusual for her to be dozing upon my return. Sure enough, as I approached the car her head was down and leaning to one side. As I lightly knocked on the window she quickly looked up and unlocked the door. I said, "Were you sleeping?"

She said, "No, I was praying to the Father." That moment reminded me of what the 12-year old Jesus had said to his mother and father when they discovered Him at the synagogue after he had been missing: "Didn't you know I would be about My Father's business?"

What were *my* prayers like during some of those most difficult days? Many times I prayed that God in His mercy would simply keep me healthy so that I could continue to care for Judy. I also often asked that if He was going to call her home soon what would be the purpose if His intention was to "refine" her? The answer with which I had to settle is that God will surely keep His promise to give good gifts to her. And when I die and again ask God this question in-person I am no less certain I will fully understand and agree with His decision. Faith is the conviction of things unseen.

Our friend, Valorie, sent me a note during Valentine's week two years after Judy's diagnosis. Her words brought tears to my eyes as she shared that Judy had taught her so much—courage, joy, perseverance, purity, peace, and death." Further, she said before a room full of Stephen Ministers in April of 2007 that she had not cried so much at someone's death as at Judy's passing.

THE REAL MEANING OF MARRIAGE

The relationship between a godly husband and wife is one of the most powerful ways human beings can both glorify God and bear witness to His goodness. I have been blessed through covenant marriage twice in my life, both times with godly and loving wives. Were it not for Judy's and my marriage and commitment before God I do not know how we would have been able to sustain each other through the nineteen months of her battle with lung cancer. Further, I do not know how I would have progressed from inconsolable mourning to beginning recovery in the months following her passing if the Lord hadn't subsequently brought Helga into my life by putting her squarely in my path at our church.

Some people have the idea that marriage is some arbitrary notion conceived by mankind and thus can be construed in a variety of ways. Rather, marriage is instituted by God Himself. Do you know that the only recorded statement made prior to the fall of man was a poem actually related to marriage?

You will recall in Genesis we are told that God caused a deep sleep to fall upon Adam, and that He took one of his ribs and then closed up the flesh in its place. The rib God took from man He made into a woman. Thus, God Himself united a man and a woman in marriage! Of that circumstance Adam uttered this poem: "This is now bone of my bones and flesh of my flesh: She shall be called Woman, because she was taken out of Man."

God's Word is very explicit on the subject of marriage: "For this reason a man will leave his father and mother and be united to his wife, and they will become one flesh." Here is the bottom line: Marriage is not for His benefit, but for ours . . . *to* His glory. Further, marriage is the relationship that offers the most intimacy between two human beings, and, as R.C. Sproul puts it, "We must be careful to obey God's regulation for marriage, thus avoiding shaming one's spouse through either comments or deeds outside of a true and legal commitment." Thus marriage is a sacred covenant. Living together outside of marriage is not.

I'm hardly qualified as a marriage counselor, but I know this from my own successful experience: Both Judy and I continued—and now Helga and I continue–to become intimately familiar with one another's world, letting ourselves be influenced by each other. I received an e-mail from a friend of mine–someone who had not yet chosen to place her trust in Christ Jesus—but she had this to say in response to one of my Judy updates: "I appreciate that you can still hold onto the faith you have, given your circumstances. It causes me to ask even more questions."

This was said of B.B. Warfield, a servant of the Lord (1851-1921): "His calling was to teach, to write, and to be a caring and loving husband." Billy Graham says of true love that it has three primary defining aspects; that it is 1) self-giving, 2) sacrificial, and 3) involves putting your spouse ahead of yourself. Let me add that if people who plan to marry ever figure out what is truly important in life, there is going to be a serious oversupply of divorce attorneys.

Twice in my lifetime has the following saying applied to me: "It takes a minute to find a special person, a day to fall in love with them, but then the rest of one's life remembering them." How blessed in this life am I?

THE JOY OF SIMPLE THINGS

When Judy and I brought her weakening condition to the attention of our hospice nurse during a visit in mid-May of 2004 she responded with a question to me: "What are you going to do when Judy is unable to get up the stairs?" I began to think about that. As I did, my first reaction was that our greatly underused living room could serve no better purpose than as a bed room.

Wendi and Kevin came to visit for a few days over Judy's and my joint mid-May birthday weekend in 2005, bringing Abigail and Karsten with them. They brought a surprise birthday gift of help for some of our added living expenses, plus an even more precious gift– a video of both Abigail's first-year piano recital and her tenth annual dance recital. We had missed her dance recital that year for the first time in many years. Both Judy and I naturally found ourselves amid tears flowing from both pride and joy.

As we drove the four of them to the airport for their return, Judy became nauseous and began vomiting into the litter bag I kept in the van. Kevin gave her one heavy-duty anti-nausea sublingual wafer and then yet another. They didn't help. We quickly unloaded everyone and their bags and drove off for home. She couldn't shake the nausea, however, and halfway back I had to pull into an office building's parking lot in order to apply a wet cloth to her forehead before continuing the remaining thirty-minute drive home. Once out of the car, she quickly recovered, happy merely for being home.

Some interesting e-mails awaited our return. Some fifteen encouraging responses to my latest Judy update/newsletter had stacked up, including one which read, "Although we have never met, I am so incredibly grateful to be included in your e-mails. Your love for one another is so powerful. God's grace shines brilliantly in your lives. I am nearly at a loss for words." Judy fairly glowed as I read the letter to her. It is amazing how easy it is to uplift someone merely through a few words of encouragement.

During a Saturday afternoon solo trip to the grocery store, as I was listening to my favorite Christian talk radio station, I heard about a man who had just been made president of a prestigious university and was at the peak of his career when his wife was diagnosed with Alzheimer's. He then gave an address at the university at which he said that his wife had given him so many wonderful years that the least he could do was give her "these years." He resigned to do exactly that. Well, having joyfully given Judy "these years" of my life was never a "decision" I had to make. It was merely an extension or our lives and a loving opportunity to serve. Through her devotion and love for me and our children she had already given me many more.

Judy's hospice social worker was always very solicitous and helpful. As I invited her into the house one day and began following her into the family room where Judy was sitting, I heard her say, "I brought my wedding pictures." With that I made an abrupt U-turn and went outside to pitch horseshoes. Judy was interested, however, simply because she took a joyful interest in whatever interested others. Frankly, I could use more of that quality, but then when it comes to looking at a casual acquaintance's wedding pictures doesn't a man have to draw the line somewhere?

IT'S NOT ABOUT ME

One afternoon Satan planted some self-pitying thoughts in my mind. They went something like this: "What has my life become that I can no longer travel to see family or friends, regularly attend church services, or participate in an overnight men's Christian retreat, not to mention getting in a round of golf? Poor me." I quickly understood what was happening, however, and literally rebuked Satan in Christ's name, adding that life wasn't about me, but about serving God and others. And at that particular time it was especially about serving Judy. As you and I serve our spouses—or for that matter, serve anyone—we serve the Lord Himself.

Isn't is easy to forget that life is short, no matter how many years we live? We need to live for God today, and that means living in such a way that we draw nearer to Him. In that way He will draw nearer to us and no matter when our lives end, we will have fulfilled God's plan for us. The last thing we want is for Jesus to have to rebuke us as He once found necessary in speaking quite literally to James and John when they were looking to be placed at either side of Jesus in heaven. He said to them in quite literal fashion, "You Sons of Zebudee!"

One day a former business colleague called me with the news that his wife needed to be admitted to hospice care. He wanted a recommendation for that as well as for a support group for himself, and prayer for both of them. In addition to offering what I could in each of those regards I also suggested he get himself plugged into a church. I included an invitation to attend church with us, but h e never availed himself of that or many other subsequent invitations. To this day he has no real support system and well over two years later still finds himself mired in the grieving process. I believe he could be characterized as being focused more on survival than on healing.

A much more positive opportunity for encouragement came in the form of a fellow Stephen Minister and her fearfully ailing husband. Her husband would pass away from cancer within a year of Judy's being called home. The husband was a faithful child of God and went to his heavenly reward with certainty for the everlasting hope of immortality in God's presence. A few months after his passing Helga and I asked his widow to join us for dinner at our home. During the evening she noticed a flower vase she had given Judy when she and her husband had served us about two years earlier in bringing dinner to our home. She had come to grips with her circumstances and welcomed the challenge of healing and learning to live alone after so many years of a successful, loving marriage.

The loss of my loved one brings to my mind a few stanzas of an anonymous poem that speak to grief and mourning from the perspective of the departed one. Their beautiful words read like this: "Don't grieve for me, for now I'm free. I'm following the path God laid for me. Perhaps my time seemed all too brief. Don't lengthen it now with undue grief."

Jason and Wheng came to visit and shared with us about his seemingly never-ending travel in the work he otherwise enjoys. Wheng excitedly told us of her raise, the second in the one year she had been on the job. But she also told us of an incident of harassment by two men whose work she recently began overseeing. She let the first incident go, but the harassment increased, and she finally reported the incidents. As a result of management's warning to them they changed their tune and all was well. Judy was so interested in their sharing that it gave her a special lift.

One particular morning Judy had a rare look of resignation about her and I asked her how she was feeling. She said, "I'm not complaining, but I don't feel at all well." I asked her if she would like a Zofran, a high-powered anti-nausea medicine. I detected a slight head nod, but at the same time she said, "I'm not supposed to be taking those." She was referring to the fact that the pills were

$32 a pop and we had no prescription insurance. She felt she had to be judicious in their use. I immediately placed one under her tongue and within fifteen minutes she felt enough better to ask for two cups of her chocolate soy shake!

On Memorial Day weekend, 2005, as I sat on Judy's footstool in front of her sleep chair in the bedroom living room at 2:00 A.M., I could tell she was lightly sleeping. I had just changed both her inside and outside sleep-shirt towels and she said, brightly, "Hey, we have a pretty good pit crew!" I laughed out loud at how her comment had struck me, being the big race weekend and all.

The next day we were prompted to take a humorous "Dementia" test, which had been sitting on my desk for several days. Of the five questions, I missed four. Judy only missed one. Later in the week, my mother—who was actually suffering from mild dementia–correctly answered all of them!

Then we received really good news. Martin and Betty came over to celebrate her 36th birthday and she mentioned they had a picture they wanted us to see. The picture wasn't a print, however, but a sonogram of their eight-week old fetus! I cried into both Betty's and Martin's arms, overjoyed for them as well as for us. Judy was so happy she immediately began talking about how she had been praying for so long for their yet-to-be-conceived child. When we spoke of the due date, however, I could see momentary sadness in Judy's eyes. We would continue to pray for the baby during the remainder of the pregnancy, but the baby would not be born until nearly four months after Judy passed away.

I went to Northside Hospital in Atlanta to visit my friend Bob following his hip replacement surgery.

He was bed-bound for the day and as reward for my loyalty in visiting he allowed me to both hold and empty his urinal tube!

Judy's hospice nurse came to visit and brought the bad news that she was being promoted and would be more of a troubleshooter than a regular. Interestingly, she also told us she had reservations about the promotion, even suggesting that if we weren't happy with it she would welcome our calling the executive director.

I did so, registering our complaint at the instability of having to work with a third primary hospice nurse in six months. At the same time I was careful to compliment all of the staff with whom we had come in contact. He said he would see what he could do about her staying with us as well as taking on the new promotion duties. Within another week that is exactly what happened.

I went to the hospital once again to check on Bob as he was being given two units of blood. I wanted to pray with him but didn't bring it up. The last time I had offered to do so he refused to allow it. I think it was more my fault in that the way I offered he may have thought I was asking *him* to pray.

The week ended with a neighbor bringing over a beautiful blue-and-purple refill from her flower garden for Judy's Hydrangia bowl. They were able to talk about life, family and friendships. Before long her husband would not only express interest in joining our Saturday Bible study, but become a regular and valuable addition to the group.

HOPE ABOUNDS

To you married folk I say what greater God-given privilege than to cheerfully servant one's wife or husband? The many months since Judy's diagnosis I considered to be grace from God. I savored every moment with her. I grew in my relationship with Jesus, just as Judy and I grew closer together in ways different than before. As important as it is for a man to become a successful father, he can achieve no greater accomplishment than to first become a successful husband.

In any given week Judy seemed to have to fight some or all of the various bogeys loosed upon her by–or in conjunction with–her cancer: Crackling or diminished capacity lungs, fitful upright sleeping, severe weakness, nausea, searing needle-like pain from sinusitis, constipation, and a wracking, watery cough. We couldn't decide for ourselves which was worse. As weak and exhausted as she was, however, she was never too diminished for communion with the Lord or for enjoyment of her precious family.

Surprisingly, at the 16-month mark she had begun displaying a renewed, if modest, appetite. She even put me on a regular two-restaurant circuit to pick up take-out egg drop soup and chicken and dumplings. One day, after I returned from my take-out run I told her I had become such a regular customer at the two restaurants that they had begun deducting payroll taxes from the change they gave me!

Whimsy aside, I had by then come to fully understand that her suffering and my challenge were not punishment for our sins, but pruning, beneficial to us to God's glory. And all of that comes down to an understanding that if the second Adam—Christ—had to suffer for our sins–and He did in order for us to be forgiven by a Holy God–then we may also suffer (to one extent or another) to His glory.

These aren't my ideas, understand. They are Biblical. In Peter 4:12-13 we are reminded that rather than be surprised at trials, we should rejoice in them. I understand that for many this is a very hard lesson. We rejoice, however, because those who believe in Christ Jesus have been counted worthy to suffer for Him, whether through persecution for our faith or through the common trials of life. This doesn't mean I didn't pray to God in the name of Jesus to restore Judy's health, if it be His will. I did, endlessly.

Through all the trials connected with Judy's battle–trials that drained her, pained her, and tested not only her stamina, but her will and her faith in our Lord and Savior—we took encouragement from a very special admonishment from Paul in his letter to the Corinthians. These verses are read from *The Message's* translation in 2 Corinthians 6:4-10 and they are words I read again and again: "People are watching us as we stay at our post (voluntarily trusting in the Lord, even if we don't fully understand), alertly, unswervingly . . . immersed in tears, yet always filled with deep joy . . ."

And in John 14:14 there is yet another mysterious lesson for us: "If you ask for something in my name, I will do it." In David Stern's JNT commentary he succinctly explains the broader concept of this extraordinary verse. He notes that Jesus is telling His disciples: "You are my followers; and the Father has given me authority to receive your requests, which are at once communicated to Him. He has also given me authority to grant your requests . . . (for) asking Me is the same as asking Him. If your requests are godly, in accord with God's plan, I will fulfill them."

What incredible comfort is derived from the above. As Oswald Chambers put it: "As Christians we are not here for our own purpose at all–we are here for the purpose of God, and the two are not the same . . ." People's lives may go on for many, many years or last only a few more hours. No one knows. We do well to use this knowledge as a motivation to work diligently so that we might leave a legacy that produces fruit for the kingdom long after we are gone. Judy certainly left such a legacy.

Growing up, I heard my father exclaim many times, "Man does not live by bread alone!" He used the phrase most commonly on the golf course. As I would caddy for him he often made this reference relative to a good recovery shot having been made following a lousy shot which preceded it. I did not realize until much later in life the significance of the *full* verse: "Man does not live by bread alone, but by every word that proceeds from the mouth of God." Quite a different context, wouldn't you say?

FOR THE LOVE OF GOD

I have a fair-sized magnet on the back of my car which reads *Love God, Love People*. It has been there since the Spring of '06 when our church distributed them in concert with our senior pastor's sermon on the subject. I still see them on cars all over the Roswell-Alpharetta-Cumming area. The elemental message was and is this: If we love God then we must also love our neighbors as ourselves. Who is your neighbor? Anyone you might reasonably be able to comfort in one fashion or another. While this is easy to say, for most of us it is not easy to do. At least it is not easy to do most of the time, but I think that is the point.

I used to think I was allowed to make a distinction between liking someone and loving them. I mean there were people I would just as soon "God bless with a brick" (to borrow a phrase from a friend). But I have since been convicted not to make such a distinction. Look how much God loves each and every one of us in spite of our unloveliness. That doesn't mean everyone He loves is saved, but He truly desires everyone to love Him, to change their heart, and to ask forgiveness.

A former senior pastor of our church wrote in an e-mail letter to me, "I trust in the ultimate goodness and will of God." He was referring to his own difficulties in the death of his and his wife's adult child who died among the 110 people in the May , 1996 Florida plane crash. In conclusion he wrote, "I know in a little while I will see him again. Time is slow of foot, but eternity is immediate. In a moment, we will be together again." I have thought about that and the meaning of those words. I believe the point of it is that since eternity extends both backward and forward without end—with our lives on this earth represented by a mere pencil point on that line with no end—the time (within the framework of eternity) between now and a reunion with a lost loved one is literally "but a moment."

Judy loved to both read and hear good, clean jokes. At her suggestion I submitted our favorite "believer-category" joke to *Reader's Digest*. As for me, I told the joke many times, both within the context of a faith presentation and to family and friends. I include it here because I suspect Judy may still be telling it at the "new admissions" desk in heaven. The story involves two fellow believers—a Messianic rabbi and a Catholic priest—in a discussion about the possibilities for promotion within the church for today's youth.

The priest was telling the rabbi that his nephew would shortly be graduating from seminary and with a little time was reasonably assured of a promotion to clergyman. The rabbi nodded and said, "And then what?" The priest said, "Well, if he does a good job he'll surely be promoted to chaplain." The rabbi, obviously not impressed, repeated himself with, "And then what?"

The priest, a little irritated, responded with, "Well, he has both a good head and a faithful heart, my friend, so Bishop isn't too hard to imagine." The rabbi again responded with, "And then what?" By then the priest was more than a little upset and he stammered as he shot back, "Okay, so maybe he could make Archbishop and then, who knows, maybe even Cardinal. Yeah!"

The rabbi's eyebrows inched up but he stayed with the same line, "And then what?" The priest was nearly beside himself in exasperation, but he persevered, exclaiming with a note of finality, "Well, Rabbi . . . you know . . . *someone* has to be pope." The rabbi stared him down, and with a smug look asked the same question one last time: "And then what?"

At that the priest threw both of his hands up into the air and shouted, "What do you think, man? That he could become God?" The rabbi folded his hands and said softly, "Well, one of *our* boys made it."

TIME BECOMES MORE PRECIOUS

Judy and I watched a movie on CD, Bobby Darin's story, *Beyond The Sea*. About halfway through the film I put it on pause in order to take a break. That was right after Darin's health situation had been clearly established. While I was out of the room I realized how related that scene was to Judy's terminal illness and immediately began to weep. Before I returned, I asked Jesus to take my hand.

The final scene came which, in my opinion, was so very well-written and creatively staged; i.e., Darin— knowing he was singing for the last time in public—exited the stage following his killer performance, only to be immediately put on oxygen. My emotions flooded up and overcame me. I put my hands to my mouth as tears welled up and out of my eyes. Judy immediately reached to comfort me. We embraced without words.

My last Father's Day to be spent with Judy was a fine day. I consumed nearly an entire butterscotch pie, just one of the many treats I often employ in ignoring my sugar addiction. That night was again very difficult for Judy but, wonder of wonders, the next morning she was very alert and we spent an hour and a half talking and laughing.

We focused on the Summer of 1956 when we first met while working for the same company in our hometown in Iowa. She in order-processing and I in the factory. I had asked one of her friends in the mail room to tell me about her, but then made the mistake of telling her friend I thought Judy was a bit "silly" (obviously a poor choice of words but I had seen her clowning around on a tour of the factory and thought both the clowning and she were cute). Judy's friend shared my comment with her! She laughed it off, but after we had been married for several months the circumstances leading up to my investigation of her through her friend and my use of the "silly" word came up again as we were washing the dinner dishes. The consequences of that earlier faux pas finally managed to catch up with me as I caught a dripping wet dishcloth full in the face!

Judy's long-time hairdresser called to say she could take her right away if I would bring her to the shop. Her only hairdo in the previous 17 months had been at our home with my barber. We went and I stayed with her the entire time for her wash, a short cut, and style. She never stopped smiling and I never stopped watching her smile.

One night I was suddenly awakened by a sharp, unfamiliar sound. I looked up to find Judy standing in front of her dresser with a drawer opened. Sleepily, I asked what she was doing. She said, "I need a fresh lid." I didn't know what she was talking about, so I repeated my question. She said, "You know, a dry nightshirt." After we both had a good laugh I saw to outfitting her with a fresh 'lid.'

As Judy became less and less able to get around away from the house, I went to visit a nearby store which sold electric scooters. The next Saturday the sales rep followed up by coming to our home and bringing along the one I liked and thought we could afford. After a full demo with an excited Judy at the tiller in our kitchen and hallway, we opted to buy it. The sales rep was not only very helpful but he asked about the yard sign I had left up after my MOW group had come and gone earlier that day.

The sign I'm referring to read, "Men Meeting Here in the Name of Jesus Christ." I asked him if he was a believer. We then spent the next twenty minutes talking about the Lord's work in each of our lives. After he left I suggested to Judy that she name the scooter. She came up with "Gracie," out of respect for God's exceeding grace and mercies toward us. Gracie would become an integral part of our lives for another two months.

I picked up Wendi, Abigail and Karsten (WAK) at the airport for a few days's visit. Abigail and I took a short walk down by the lake and I talked to her about her grandmother's condition, concluding our time with the thought that our trust in the Lord was a part of our obedience to Him. Our nearly thirteen-year-old was maturing practically before our eyes. She understood.

As for the barely seven-year old Karsten, when I went into his room the next morning to awaken him he held out his arms to me just as he had the first morning spent in this country, nearly five years earlier. He looked up at me that very first night, his eyes twinkling as he waited to uplift his arms until someone in authority okayed it. That, of course, was a carryover from his time only a few days earlier when he had still been in the Russian orphanage. Judy and I talked about that time in our lives and marveled at God's miracle in having brought him so lovingly into our children's–and our—lives.

As a sidebar to the notion of adoption, it is interesting to relate to our own adoption by God through the shed blood of Christ. In biblical times it was customary for a father to "adopt" a son whom he thought especially worthy of his blessing. As believers we are therefore God's preferred sons and daughters, heirs of the Kingdom.

Judy's Stephen Minister's step-father passed away unexpectedly and I went to his memorial service. Things went okay for me until I hugged Valorie at grave side. She said, "I can't believe you came. I know how hard this must be for you." It was. Before I left the cemetery I stopped to check on Judy's and my pre-set cremation bench. Granite does quite well without much attention.

TRANSFORMING TRUTHS

When I sent out my 17-month Judy update in July of '05 I mentioned that her hands were so weak she couldn't squeeze toothpaste from a tube. But through that extreme weakness she nevertheless continued to encourage and inspire others through her trust and faith in the Lord God. We asked for strength and He gave us difficulties to make us strong. We asked for wisdom and He gave us problems to solve. And though we did not receive what we wanted, we did receive everything we needed.

On Judy's good days she was absolutely radiant in both her countenance and her counsel. I jokingly told her I thought she could give hope to a goat. Helen Keller once said that so much had been given her she had no time to ponder over that which had been denied. Ditto, Judy Dodd.

With reference to the "transforming truths" article in my newsletter, the first truth I made reference to was the popular cliche which asserts that "All religions are valid." The problem with this concept is clearly stated by David Catchpoole in a *Creation* magazine article in which he wrote, "All truths can be equal only if none are really true."

The second transforming truth I shared dealt with the question, "How important is it to know truth?" Well, by faith we can identify ourselves with Noah and the seven others whom alone God considered righteous and worthy of saving from the flood. He brought total destruction upon the world of the ungodly and, as *Tabletalk* magazine so succinctly puts it, "If God preserved the righteous before, we can be confident He will do it again."

The flip side of that is equally critical: God punishes those who will not acknowledge Him in this life in the worst possible way. He turns them over to sin even further. Concerning this same point Psalms 14:1 says, "The fool has said in his heart, 'There is no God.'" I favor one Bible translation's commentary in particular, which explains, "Whether you acknowledge God's existence is not the question. Even demons believe in God, but their 'belief' makes them tremble, because they know they cannot avoid His punishment for their evil deeds and thoughts."

The good thing about the bad news of the above second truth, however, comes with the understanding that there is actually a way to be declared not guilty! What more important words have ever been written than those in Romans 3:21 which tell us that righteousness from God comes through faith in Christ Jesus, to . . . *all* . . . who believe.

Of all the material I digested in putting together my journal notes for this book I don't think anything more clearly presents this third and last transforming truth (the washing away of our sins for those who believe in Him) as does an article in *Zion's Fire* magazine by longtime missionary Marion Rosenthal. I have taken certain literary liberties with her presentation, but have not altered her message.

Visualize three beings in two different scenarios. The first scenario features God the Father, God the Son, and a lost sinner. The second scenario involves the Father, the Son, and another sinner, but one who believes God's Word.

In the first scenario the sinner is one who has never repented of his sin. His hopes of going to heaven depend entirely upon the good things he has done in his lifetime. This is a sinner–even as you and I are–but he never repented of his sin.

He is now standing—eye-to-eye–before a holy God. He will either admit him to heaven or not. Before the truth prevails we first need to understand what God has already made quite clear through His Word, and that is this: "Not by works of righteousness which we have done, but according to his mercy he saved us" (Titus 3:5).

So, here stands the sinful man, one who had never availed himself of Christ's payment for man's sin, the very salvation God the Son died to provide for his cleansing and forgiveness. What is God to say? He who loves him yet sees him in all of his sin. Can God allow unholiness to enter into His holy heaven? Again: "Not by works of righteousness which we have done, but according to his mercy he saved us." Sadly but simply, the sin remains condemned. To me, the implication of that judgment is clear.

Enter scenario number two: In this instance the sinner/believer agreed with God that she was a sinner and needed a Redeemer—One who paid the penalty for her sin and One who forgave her when she repented–who now became her Savior and Lord. Again, the sinner stands before a holy God, but with one huge difference. She is not eye-to-eye with God the Father. What has happened? Simply this. The Messiah Jesus stands between her and a holy God. Christ has placed Himself between the two! How does that change things? Based on the redemptive work of His Son, the Father forgives and sends the Holy Spirit to wash away our sins and continually renew us.

Thus, the third truth–and the truth of all truths—is that God looks at a forgiven sinner and sees His Son. How that changes things! Christ's intercession makes the sinner acceptable before a God who has "purer eyes than to behold evil" (Habbukuk 1:13). Here, then, is the ultimate transforming question: On what basis should God let you or me into His holy heaven?

THIS IS YOUR LIFE

As our hospice nurse came to see Judy she informed us that of the fifteen patients she was seeing, mostly twice a week, Judy was the only one not bed-bound. Further, she said that Judy was the only one who talked of her faith in—and service to—the Lord.

On the cover of this book it is written that whatever your tough lesson in life—be it the loss of a loved one, divorce, a drug or alcohol addiction, deep depression, a debilitating illness, or any one of a long list of physical, emotional or spiritual issues that cause heartache—God is the answer. In other words–in this vein–Judy and I had this to say: "This is what has come upon us, Father in heaven. We don't know how or why, but we unconditionally trust in you."

While God does not actually deliver us *from* our difficulty, he nevertheless delivers us *in* it, if we but have faith in Him. Moreover–in the words of one poetic author–"In the process of enduring God's refining fires, He allows us to shed the slag of life."

THE STRUGGLE INTENSIFIES

After I finished washing Judy's hair one afternoon she stepped back from the kitchen sink, paused and said, "I am so grateful to God. Let's sit and tell him about it for a few minutes." Could anyone deny such a graceful invitation as that?

My July 15, 2005 journal begins with this entry: "What a day: Beautiful sunlight and no nausea! Beyond that, Mike Roper came to our home late this morning to bring communion and to pray with us."

That same day, following lunch, Judy and I and RAWBi (now more thoughtfully adorned with two pigtails, thanks to our granddaughter) found ourselves aboard our van, along with Gracie. Off we went to market.

Once inside The Fresh Market, with Judy aboard Gracie, she slowly maneuvered up and down the aisles. Her countenance was one of awe at her relative freedom. She was out and about and carefully selecting fresh vegetables here and special salads there, never breaking her smile. I don't know which made me happier, the joy on her face or the fact that we were actually out grocery shopping together.

My good friend Bob had called and wanted me to go to the health club with him later that afternoon. I told him I couldn't make that decision until after we returned from our outing and subject to how Judy was doing. When we returned she seemed to think it would be okay if I went. And so I did. Bob needed some help to get into the pool, and didn't actually swim, but walked the length of the pool four or five times as I swam alongside him. When we exited the building it was raining hard so I fetched my car and picked him up at the club curb to drive him the twenty yards to his own car so he wouldn't have to wade through standing water with his walker. Both his physical and emotional health were sliding noticeably.

I don't know exactly how to convey the level to which Judy's own health had deteriorated during that week except to say there was a marked difference. One Saturday morning after the Men of the Way had left, I checked on her and she was sleeping as she sat leaning forward in her chair. Her oxygen nosepiece was out of position, foam (from involuntary gurgling) was on her lips and nose, and both her neck towel and waterproof vest were soaked to the point that I could have wrung out a pint of water from them. When I gently took one of her hands from under the sheet that covered her it was very cold, even given the July heat of the day. She opened her eyes and said, weakly, "Are your guys gone? How many came?" What grace from God that a dying person could be so selfless?

After cleaning her up and holding her hand for some time I went downstairs and cried out for God to help us. I could barely get her to stay awake. It was obvious to me that Judy was close to needing a new level of attention. The next morning, however, she had improved such that after lunch she wanted to go with me to get some groceries!

I parked in a handicapped spot facing away from the sun so that the back of the van would be shaded while I unloaded and assembled Gracie's five disassembled parts. The stuff we needed would take only fifteen minutes to pick up but Judy was having so much fun motoring up and down the aisles of the Kroger store and looking at all the new products on the shelves that we were there for over an hour. She had not been to an actual supermarket for over a year. She was still tentative at the controls and selected a scooter icon-speed halfway between "turtle" and "rabbit." I called it "tur-bit" power.

Once home, I took an e-mail from a former Iowa high school friend–then living in the Houston, TX area—whom neither Judy nor I had seen or spoken with in over 35 years. He wrote that he had been sharing my Judy updates with his weekly men's Bible study and that they had been greatly helped by her faith.

One afternoon, our long-time next-door neighbor brought us some fresh Florida tomatoes from he and wife's trip south. The same day a much newer neighbor brought us some homemade muffins. A third neighbor brought us a delicious dessert. And yet a fourth neighbor brought Judy a bouquet of flowers when she picked up a UPS package from us I had intercepted on her behalf. The widow had been gone amid a downpour that would have likely ruined any package left on her doorstep. She had lost her husband some few years earlier to a heart attack and was now having problems with both a balky computer and a wall leak. All I could do in that regard was look up two phone numbers for her whose "yellow pages" ad promised to be able to help. As Judy had pointed out to me so often through her own witness, no one should have to fight their battle alone.

Judy's oxygen saturation level was measuring 86%. This means her body was using only 86% of the oxygen it received. My blood oxygen, by comparison, usually ranges from 97% to 100%. Even my mother, fighting COPD, usually managed to register 94% oxygen saturation. Interestingly, the fact that Judy's nose-drips and her wet-cough spitting brought up a significant volume of water through the course of a day and night was of benefit to her. Since her cancer-attacked body had been generating so much water, all of the cavities available to her would have been filled if she weren't also draining water.

Through all of this Judy was growing in sanctification every day. That is, she was growing to be more like Christ. Think about this in relation to the difficult lessons in each of our lives. Without adversity how *would* one become more like the suffering servant? Through trials and testings of our own, God is perfecting His holiness within us that you and I might better reflect the glory and beauty of the Lord Jesus Christ. But exactly how does this work? Through hardship and suffering don't we lean more heavily on Him and find Christ to be sufficient for our every need?

FORE!

I heard from my youngest brother as he responded to my suggestion that we initiate funeral pre-planning for our mother. He okayed everything with the semi-joking comment that he didn't necessarily think he would outlive her, given his end-stage emphysema. He told me of his own, very different pre-planning, which included something I at first thought was a total joke. It wasn't. He wants his cremated ashes to be given to his two sons for their use in filling divots on a round of golf! If that should actually happen I think the story would certainly be worthy of *Golf Digest*!

Judy and I had a minor tiff one morning over how to deal with the swelling in her feet and legs. For some reason I thought she might not be taking her Lasix pills. I wanted her to take the pill while I was watching. She felt I didn't trust her to take it. I quietly left the room with the pill still in my hand, but we later smoothed things over. The point is that we tried never to let even minor disagreements go unresolved.

A day or so later Judy felt up to my being gone for a few hours so that I could attend my Monday evening's Stephen Ministry continuing education. There, I offered encouragement for a fellow minister who was quite nervous about presenting the evening's devotion. I had made up an Olympic-style "10" sign and held it up just as she finished. Everyone laughed, but she did quite well without my encouragement.

One afternoon Judy decided she wanted to go to Wal-Mart. RAWBi was thus towed behind the grocery cart, which , in turn, was hooked onto the back of Gracie. Two little kids stopped in the aisle and giggled, apparently fascinated by the entourage. I think they were particularly taken with the Sesame Street nightgown-clothed character (Ernie) which RAWBi wore as she faced rearward from the cart.

The downer of the day was a call from an Iowa aunt who told us my uncle had passed away earlier that day. He was taken only two months from the time of his cancer diagnosis. That was a reminder of how precious Judy and I could look at the previous eighteen months as Grace from God, regardless of her continuously failing health.

One afternoon *Moonlight Serenade* was playing on the TV's music channel. I asked Judy if she wanted to dance but she smiled in demurring. She was sitting on the couch so I simply bent over and placed each of her hands in mine and my cheek next to hers. We "danced" through the remainder of the song without her leaving the sofa.

Why did she continue to fight so through her pain? Because she willed to do God's will. She could yet work to His glory through her attitude, her words, and her actions. If God is always in control–and He is–then not only was Judy exactly where He wanted her to be but when He did finally call she would know that she had been faithful to the end.

I began to think in earnest about how I would care for her when her condition worsened to the point of requiring around-the-clock care. In the end I couldn't resolve that and simply turned it over to God.

WHY DID GOD MAKE ME?

One day I tried to install a new toner cartridge in one of my computer printers but couldn't get the job done properly. I readily admit to being somewhat dyslexic when it comes to following printed "some assembly required" directions. Therefore, I had always relied upon Judy to fix office stuff. Sure enough, after about an hour at that particular challenge I went upstairs to plead my case, saying, "Please get well so you can take back this job!" Naturally, she quickly fixed it. How pathetic am I?

Our current hospice nurse had come for one of her twice-weekly visits and since my stomach had been almost continuously upset for more than a week, I asked her advice. She suggested some over-the-counter med like Pepcid. She also added a suggestion that I hire an assisted living at-home person to stay with Judy for four hours one afternoon a week in order to give me some downtime. I said I would look into that.

I phoned a new referral to our MOW group and invited him to attend the following Saturday. He said he would and did. He stayed afterwards for a while and shared with me the challenges he was facing in life. He stayed with the group for nearly six months and I felt that during that time he found some new friends who were interested in both him and his needs.

As Judy and I talked about many different things while she was trying to "find" her legs one morning, we discussed something of the dreams we had each recently experienced. We rarely talked about our dreams and she reminded me that she prayed nightly not to have any conscious or subconscious dreams about family. Her reasoning was that such dreams often reflect particular concerns and then they grow, usually totally beyond reality. She wanted only Godly dreams and thoughts. God apparently answered her prayers in that regard as she never complained of any dream problems.

She was having other problems, however, and the hospice nurse suggested I make up a sign for the house reading something like, "Thank you for visiting Judy. For her health, please, no hugs." I did exactly that, posting the sign at the entrance to the family room where most of her time on the main floor was spent. Non-family visitors naturally wanted to hug her, but that offered more potential harm than help because her immune system was tremendously depleted.

I began reading about ways in which God uses suffering in our lives. Some of the more meaningful to me were: 1) It is only when you are weakened–that is, not dependent upon yourself–that you can be strong in Christ. 2) He has said that His grace is sufficient for us. 3) Because God can comfort us in the midst of our suffering, we will be able to comfort others with the same comfort, giving them hope.

4) Often, people with the greatest character have usually either experienced tragedies or walked a path of suffering. 5) We had the sentence of death placed within us in order that we should not trust in ourselves, but in God who raises the dead and will yet deliver those who believe in Him. 6) If Christ suffered for us (pierced, afflicted, and forsaken, to name only a few), doesn't our own suffering change our perspective on what Christ did for us?

7) The Lord giveth and the Lord taketh away. This one was particularly difficult for me to manage at the time. Yet, as one author puts it, when everything in us screams at the heavens for allowing suffering, we have reason to look at the eternal outcome and joy of Jesus who in His own suffering on an executioner's cross cried, "My God, My God, why have You forsaken Me?" (Matthew 27:46).

One other way God uses suffering in our lives directly lends itself to the title of this book. God has allowed suffering in our lives so that we will learn from it–a divine, purposeful opportunity for growth and change.

As I think about how Judy has impacted my life and living as well as those of her family, friends — and even strangers–I realize the truth of this final statement. And for those who might counter with, "The lesson didn't do *her* much good!" Again, I say, "How can you presume to know how God rewards His devoted children?" This life of ours is merely our short-term bodily life and hardly representative of everlasting life in Christ.

I received a phone call inquiring about my interest in ghost-writing a quickie 300-word article for the association magazine of which I had been a member for about twenty years. The sales manager of one of their industry supplier advertisers was not up to writing it and was willing to pay to have the work done. I shared the inquiry with Judy. I was reluctant to follow up but she encouraged me to accept the work, which I then did. I also managed to include within the article the barest of a witness to the Father's work in people's lives, but I suspect that was edited out. I never saw the printed version.

In closing this section on why God made us, let me relate a short story that perfectly makes the point. One day, a little boy asked his mother, "Why did God make me?" She replied thoughtfully, "He didn't *make* you, son. He is *making* you now." While we yet live in this life it is important to know that God is not through making *any* of us.

LOVE SHINES THROUGH

One Saturday morning a Jewish friend of mine shared with our MOW group something of his volunteer evangelizing efforts around the world. I mentioned him in an earlier section where he and I attended a rabbinic talk that would supposedly address Jesus as the Messiah. My friend is a self-described Christian witness to the Jewish people and he has traveled the world in trying to reach Jews. I am always amazed at his boldness to walk into a rabbinic synagogue (the veritable lion's den) whenever he is invited. Once there, he seeks out opportunities to witness (but only when asked what he does). Once that gate has been opened he is not bashful in sharing, full in the knowledge that more times than not he will either be asked out or literally thrown out for his "blasphemy." He is not ashamed of the Gospel.

When our home health-care person arrived to sit with Judy while I went to church it wasn't long before Judy had told her that she was a prayer warrior with our church. She asked if there was anything about which she could pray for her sitter. The lady said, yes, that her dream as one of eleven children was to continue her schooling towards achieving her lifelong goal of becoming a pediatrician. Judy said she felt so privileged to be asked to pray with her for such a worthy ambition.

The hospice nurse came to visit one mid-morning rather than her usual mid-afternoon to "see Judy at her relative worst with respect to how she feels." She was in for a surprise. The nurse had some problems of her own, including a tooth infection. Judy immediately asked if she could pray for her, and did so on the spot. The longtime veteran hospice nurse later told me she was amazed at Judy's will. She said she didn't think she would have made it nearly as long as she had without her faith in the Lord.

I drove across the county to a Christian bookstore Judy and I had once visited and which maintained a good Messianic section. I wanted to buy a Mezuzah (a small door fixture containing a tiny printing of the Torah) for an upcoming family birthday. In the process I noticed a publishing house sale offering a special paperback edition of the New King James Bible for one dollar each! I bought twenty. The purpose of the publisher's promotion was to "give away" one million Bibles in 2005. Judy and I would ultimately purchase and give away 100 of them as our share in the effort. Almost all of them would be to those visiting our home, from plumber and HVAC technician to medicine delivery person.

Judy and I possessed our own "scud missile." That is what we called the ugly olive-drab four-foot tall emergency (24-hour) oxygen tank sitting in the living room corner. We had not had occasion to use its ugly self, but it was one of three redundant resources I maintained in the house in case of oxygen failure. The other two were the hard-wired house generator (in case of electricity failure) and the small, two-hour supply oxygen tanks designed for mobility purposes. One night her oxygen concentrator failed and we had to employ the ugly Scud for the rest of the night. By mid-morning the next day, when she again had oxygen piping into her lungs, she said, "Hey, we have lift-off!" As the replacement-Scud delivery guy was about to leave he accepted my gift of a promotional Bible and a short blessing.

Although I pray for wisdom in knowing what God calls me to do I don't always understand His answers. Like most people I prefer objective answers. I read something very interesting by Renald Showers in a *Foundations of Faith* article on his thoughts about God and wisdom: "Just as words are the outward revelation of invisible human thoughts to other human beings, so the incarnated Jesus Christ is the outward revelation of the invisible God and His wisdom to human beings."

I love what Jeremiah has to say about the Word of God. In the book bearing his name (20:9), he says, "But if I say, 'I will not mention him or speak any more in his name,' his word is in my heart like a fire, a fire shut up in my bones. I am weary of holding it in; indeed, I cannot."

SHUTTING DOWN

As the end of August 2005 neared Judy and I had a date for an outing to The Fresh Market. By 1:00 P.M. she felt so poorly that she was nearly in tears about not feeling up to going. I said we could wait for another hour to make the decision. At 2:15 she said, "Let's go."

Off we went, Judy, RAWBi, Gracie and I. The trip was so joyful for me to watch her once again–for what would be her final public outing—putt down store aisles inspecting the variety and appeal of many different fresh foods. Once again I could sense that she reveled merely in the freedom to be able to do such a simple thing. Tears welled up in my eyes. She had such an innocent expression on her face, as if to say, "I have no expectation save to live in and for the Lord through these last days, thankful for His mercies."

My friend Bob called to ask if I could come over to help him with his computer. He may have been the only one on earth whom I could actually help with a computer problem!

That night was especially difficult for Judy and at 4:00 A.M. she became so agitated she ripped off all of her gurgling-protective vests and towels and asked me not to reattach them. I gave her some Morphine, along with a Zofran. Within half an hour she settled down and was up to watching televised reports with me of Hurricane Katrina's coming ashore.

The next day the hospice nurse, Judy, and I were talking about the continuing edema in Judy's feet and legs. The V-8 she had been drinking somehow came up in the conversation. Judy told her she usually drank two cans a day. The nurse casually asked if they were the low sodium variety. When Judy said "no" the nurse jumped up and shouted, "Hallelujah! That's the edema culprit. Each 11-oz. can contains more then 800 mg of sodium chloride!" I immediately took three unopened six-packs of V-8 back to the store for credit.

Judy had begun eating less and less. Up until that point her appetite had been generally good throughout the ordeal. Her health, however, had taken a sharp downward turn over the previous three or four days. As a result her body was calling for sleep most of each day. It became a struggle for her to even begin the process of eating her favorite and helpful morning fare; prunes! Still, she continued with her prayer life and asked that I mail a check to our church marked, "Katrina disaster relief."

When the hospice nurse next came to visit, I saw her to her car and asked, "Where are we on this journey?" She hesitated before answering, but finally said, "She has only months." It seemed to me that she simply could not bring herself to say, "weeks," which is what turned out to be the case. She also added that it would be better for Judy if she would lie down. At that I bristled, saying, " She can't!" Her reply was heartbreaking for me. She said, "Terry, she *will* have to lie down at some point."

THE DYING EXPERIENCE

How do I go about writing this segment? I can't see the page through my tears, even now, a year and a half after Judy's passing. Our hospice group had been doing a wonderful job of supporting both Judy and me in many ways. One of the toughest lessons I learned from them—from both their people and from their collateral material—was about the dying experience. I learned that death not only comes in its own time and way, but is as unique as the individual experiencing it. I didn't want the lesson.

I didn't realize that the changes in one's physical body actually begin to take place one to three months before death occurs. The actual dying process often begins within the two weeks prior to death. As with Judy, a person begins to withdraw from the world around them. No more interest in newspapers, television, or computers. Then, little interest in people, visiting neighbors, and finally even from some of those persons most loved.

I tried to grasp that last point. It comes down to a time of withdrawing from everything outside of one's self and going inside. Apparently, that's where the sorting out takes place, evaluating one's self and one's life. But inside there is only room for one. This processing is usually done with the eyes closed, which often becomes sleep. Yet, it is more than just sleep. I'm given to understand that important work is going on inside a person on a level of which "outsiders" aren't aware.

Although it seemed important to me at this stage that Judy regularly eat something I didn't realize that when a body is preparing to die it is perfectly natural that eating should stop. The taking in of food is merely the way we energize our body, keeping it going, moving, alive.

Things didn't quite go that way for Judy, however. She experienced a surge of energy in her final twelve hours, as I will document a bit later. At that time she talked clearly and alertly with me and family for some time. The books say this sort of thing amounts to spiritual energy for transition from this world to the next and is used for a time of physical expression before moving on.

Judy was fast approaching the point at which she would no longer have need of a heavy, non-functioning shell (body). That is the point at which a person is preparing to enter a new place, a new form, a new life, and a new day.

Without question the single most poignant lesson of those final days and moments came for me through a passage written by Henry Van Dyke and printed in a little hospice booklet by Barbara Karnes, an Oregon RN who has surely witnessed many such ordeals as mine. For those assured of their salvation and who eagerly await everlasting life in the presence of God, this short litany—*Gone From My Sight*—is incredibly encouraging, both for the dying person and for those left behind.

GONE FROM MY SIGHT

I am standing upon the seashore. A ship at my side spreads her white sails to the morning breeze and starts for the blue ocean. She is an object of beauty and strength. I stand and watch her until at length she hangs like a speck of white cloud just where the sea and sky come to mingle with each other.

Then someone at my side says: "There, she is gone!"

"Gone where?"

Gone from my sight. That is all. She is just as large in mast and hull and spar as she was when she left my side and she is just as able to bear her load of living freight to her destined port.

Her diminished size is in me, not in her. And just at the moment when someone at my side says: "There, she is gone!" there are other eyes watching her coming, and other voices ready to take up the glad shout: "Here she comes!"

PREPARING OURSELVES

As long as I could see Judy and talk to her I could–to some extent—put aside my emotions. I continued to pray for the Lord's guidance and gently felt led to begin preparing her for what she already knew. She was more concerned, however, for everyone else, and in particular for Martin and Betty and our unborn grandchild, knowing how difficult things had been for Betty at her grandmother's recent passing.

Martin came over and explained that their doctors had assured them that, as far as her pregnancy was concerned, the stress on her would not harm the baby. It was at that time that Judy made a decision to finally accept my long-time suggestion to switch our bedroom from the second floor to the main floor. With that concession she began referring to it as our "new apartment." Her very large cup overflowed until the very end.

Wendi called to check on Judy and also tell us how proud she was of Abigail in her new school when she had recently questioned her teacher about their textbook's description of evolution's apparent fact. Her teacher declined to make a personal observation on the matter, but when asked of her own views Abigail said she believed Intelligent Design was behind man's development. Judy and I were proud grandparents!

I didn't feel like getting out my usual monthly update/newsletter but, as always, Judy lent me inspiration, saying, "You don't know but what a single person might take encouragement from something you say that wouldn't otherwise happen." Excerpts of my final newsletter before her passing follow.

SAVED FROM WHAT?

Before I finally heeded God's call to come to Him I hadn't even granted that He had been on the line. What I didn't know at the time was that He calls everyone. As my long-time best friend, Jack, indignantly said to his mother at one time in his life, as she would repeatedly witness to him, "He calls us? Calls us to *what*?" As Charles Stanley so beautifully puts the answer: "To serve almighty God."

And what if we don't heed His call? Dr. Stanley rounds out the hypothetical conversation in this fashion: "Nothing has changed. We are still called to be His servants, whether we serve or not."

Let's carry this point one bit further. Suppose you acknowledged not only that God is on the line, but that you also *knew* God wanted you to serve. You might then ask how you would know exactly what you're supposed to do about it. Well, He may simply be calling you to Himself. Would that be so terrible? I mean, suppose He didn't call at all!

JUDY'S CALL

For as long as I had known Judy she was always exceedingly kind and gentle and called to meet others where they were, full of encouragement and taking a genuine interest in them. She was more interested in listening than in talking. In my opinion her calling never changed in that regard. One thing that did change manifestly, however, was her sanctification. As the years and decades went by she truly did became more and more like Christ, just as we are all called to do. Where she had made mistakes she apologized and asked forgiveness, both from God and from those she might have wronged, however unintentionally.

Judy trusted God to do His work inside of her. She thought of what she had not as ownership, but as stewardship, and by leaning on Him she was refined even further by the fires she endured in her final months. She knew that as she grew increasingly weaker and became less dependent upon herself she was yet strengthened by her Father in heaven. From that incredible strength she reached out even further to others. Through her trust in God she was brought even closer to Him, which in turn gave her yet greater joy.

How can one have joy in one's weakest moments? Well, that's what faith teaches us. She knew she could accomplish less and less through her own strength so she more and more placed her dependence upon the Lord, who has strength for all.

My saying this might surprise you, but what Judy could accomplish on her own was actually hardly noteworthy! Yet the same goes for you and me. Because God comforted her in the midst of her suffering she was able to comfort others.

Every morning I would read to her incoming e-mails, many of which were from our church's prayer warrior leadership. And every night she would enter those prayer requests into her prayer book and take them before God. What a testimonial to Christ's teaching that we are more accurately measured by the lives we touch than by the things we have acquired in this world, or the honors bestowed by men. After all, God's two greatest commandments–and the ones from which all of the others flow–are, simply put, Love God and Love people.

In a recent Crown Financial Bible study Helga and I and our three fellow participating couples were each asked to list the benefits to the giver of his or her resources. Our Biblical reference was Matthew 6:20, which is about the storing up for ourselves treasures in heaven, where moth and rust do not destroy. One of the things I was led to write was this: "How much more beneficial is storing up for ourselves treasures in heaven than on earth, for the heavenly assets do not depreciate."

HONORING A PROMISE

Early into Judy's diagnosis I sensed God speaking to me through a short if enigmatic message. It went something like this: "Honor your promise." *Promise*, I thought at the time. *What promise?* Had I reneged on something I had promised? I didn't recall having offered our firstborn when she was still a-cooking in Judy's womb. I pondered those three words. Perhaps the "promise" had something to do with reinforcing my faith. I knew I fell far short of His wishes for me. How could a holy God possibly accept me in my condition? Well, He couldn't. That's why my only defense lay with the holy Mediator, Christ Jesus. But what had that to do with me "honoring my promise?"

I pondered things some more. What were my responsibilities in that covenant? If the human race was created to glorify God–and it was–then have I been more concerned with glorifying myself than glorifying Him? Well, I certainly had for most of my life. But I thought I had begun rectifying that. What "promise?"

If any of you needs wisdom to know what you should do, you should ask God, and He will give it to you (James 1:5). I returned God's call by praying. I asked Him again. "What promise, God?" I waited. I prayed some more. No answer. I had to shelve the question for the time being, but in the interim I strove to faithfully serve Judy in any and every way she needed. After about a year into Judy's illness I slowly began to realize something with regard to my honoring "the promise." Here's what I finally came to understand.

God had called me to glorify Him through the promise I made to my late wife on March 23, 1959. Before Him I had promised to love, honor and care for her. Not just in good times or poor, but in sickness as well as in health. What did that mean? For one thing it meant that I could not later "qualify" my promise, even though that promise had been made at the tender age of 20. Judy had certainly kept her promise to me. I was likewise responsible for my own promise. Please understand I don't mean to imply anything with respect to anyone else's situation. This was simply my personal take.

In front of Him, and in His house, I had knowingly and enthusiastically promised to love and care for my wife until death do us part. As I think about that now I am absolutely awed to have been asked by God to serve Him directly in such a fashion. When I think of the full implication of such a promise I am brought to tears. I realize that God personally loved me enough to entrust to me the care of another of His precious children for the rest of her life! And just as importantly, He hadn't called me because I was particularly equipped, rather He would equip me for His call.

I hasten to add that the Father apparently knew I would keep my promise for He has again honored me by entrusting yet another of His children to me. I will keep that trust the same as before, so help me God. Interestingly, however, I am certain He doesn't want our promises so much as our execution of those promises.

FINDING OUR WAY

In the beginning it is hard to find the Way. For most of us life becomes more difficult as we continue along the Way, and then life becomes extremely tough when we have traveled on the Way for a long time and are about to reach our final shelter . . . heaven. Yet, there is no other Way or Path for us than persevering in Christ until the end.

Martin Luther said that more than enough has been written in books about the concepts of faith, but not nearly enough has been driven into our hearts. We must trust in God alone, whether we have the resources we need or not. Trust Him, but do not test Him. Judy was ultimately made perfect through faith in Him. Not by what she did. And not before she crossed over. She received the gift of eternal and perfect life, however, simply because "she who accepts Him has everything, even conquering death" (Rom. 10:4 and Col. 2:9-10).

And how does our sin affect us? Without meaning to be judgmental, some of us hear that word and instantly become defensive with something like, "What sin? I've never killed, robbed, stolen (well, not much), fornicated (well, maybe that time or two)." While these are certainly sins, they are merely the tip of the iceberg. The fact is that most of us don't really understand the concept of sin. And many who will admit to sin still don't understand that our sinful nature is precisely why the Word became Flesh in order to save us. God knew we could not keep the Law–though it remains our guide—so by His grace was sent the Son in sacrifice for our sin.

One good definition of sin is any thought, word, action, omission, or desire that is contrary to the law or attributes of God. So, on that basis, who is a sinner? All of us. Not one of us is good. The great apostle Paul, inspired by God Himself, wrote in Romans, "For all have sinned, and come short of the glory of God." Further, it is not the *amount* or the *nature* of sin that separates a man or a woman from God and keeps him or her from Heaven, but the *fact* of sin.

Sin. What a bothersome little word; only three letters. What's the problem here? Not only is sin universal in scope and deadly in effect, it is beyond the cure of any manmade antidote. Now, not everyone agrees with this statement. In fact, notes Marvin Rosenthal (widely-read author and *Zion's Fire* magazine editor), many social scientists, educators, psychologists, and 'religious teachers' strongly disagree. So? Rosenthal points out that though many reject the concept of sin, they are disastrously wrong.

How so? Hold on to your thinking for yet awhile as you consider Rosenthal's not so delicate follow-up: "In rejecting the implications of sin, they play the fool, endanger their own eternal souls, and misguide multitudes who, in ignorance, march to their cadence."

Rosenthal points out that the first couple was fashioned in the image of God (Genesis 1:26) but chose to disobey His command (Gen. 3: 6-8). As a result, when in time they bore children, those children were born not *only* in God's image, but also in their own likeness (Gen. 5:3). Voila! Sin was thus in the loins of Adam.

IS THERE A CURE?

Only one. The cure is Jesus Christ, the Jewish Messiah. Do we mean just because He is the Savior? Well, yes, of course, but in addition to that consider Rosenthal's point that He was virgin-born and not heir to the infectious venom that gave to every son of Adam's race a sin nature, and which, in turn, manifested itself in sinful deeds. Thus, our responsibility is to believe what God has done for us through His Son, and by faith receive His free gift of salvation. Head knowledge will not do it, only heart knowledge. Mere mental assent doesn't cut it, for even demons understand who Christ is but they are not saved. Knowing *about* Christ is not the same as personally *knowing* Christ.

We are told in Psalms about believers that Christ removes our sins "as far as the east is from the west, and that that is how far He has removed our transgressions from us." Think about this phrase: *as far as the east is from the west.* I thought I knew what that meant, but I didn't fully grasp its meaning until I read Rosenthal's beautifully insightful remarks:

"The north and south poles are fixed points; if you go north far enough, you will eventually begin heading south. But there are no fixed points east and west because of the rotation of the earth. East and west are infinitely separated and will never meet." In other words, if you stay on a heading of East, you will never find yourself heading West.

Thus, it is through God's all-knowing design of creation that He also demonstrated (and illustrated) how far He has removed the transgressions of believers from those who believe. What grace and mercy!

SEPTEMBER SONG

In early September our youngest offspring took a day off work to spend it with us. Judy was overjoyed. Martin is the de facto family historian and his mother wanted him to go through several boxes of pictures with her in order to identify people for him. She had a really good afternoon.

At about 2:00 the next morning I heard Judy calling softly to me. I quickly got up from bed and she said, "Would you sit on the footstool and talk to me for a few minutes?" Although she had absolute trust in both the Lord and her fate, she was human. She needed to share and she needed comfort. That was another wonderful part of my job in our marriage. I reminded her that she was not alone, that Jesus tells us He will never leave us. Never.

We talked further. We talked about John 14:1: "Don't be troubled. Believe in God, and believe in me." A sorrowful heart doesn't come from Christ. He doesn't depress hearts. He came to this earth, did everything, and ascended into heaven to take away worry from our hearts and replace it with a cheerful heart, conscience, and mind.

Soon, Judy was ready to return to her more comfortable–if fitful—sleep position. If you can trust in what Christ says in the above passage you will be in good shape and will have won more than half the battle in dealing with whatever tough lessons in life are confronting you. Further, you will have gained in life merely through having undergone such difficult lessons. They simply aren't meant for nothing.

READINESS

A few days later the hospice chaplain was due for his appointment with Judy. I had planned to run a few errands while he was with her so I left before he arrived. I placed a note on the door explaining things, and invited him to come in as she might not be up to answering the door bell. By the time I returned he had come and gone. Judy told me she had fallen asleep and when she woke up he was holding her hand. The chaplain had his understudy with him—a very nice lady—and they talked and then prayed with her.

Early afternoon on a Friday I weighed Judy a few minutes before the nurse was due to arrive. She had dropped another five lbs. that week. The nurse found her blood pressure to be 88/58 but, more importantly, okayed her resuming the V-8 treat twice a week. That simple news thrilled her.

Her sister, Kaye, called with the news that their father had suffered a heart attack and was in ICU. After the phone call Judy became at once stoic, even somewhat defiant in saying, "I'm not ready to go yet. I want to see the baby." Then she softened her stance, saying, "But I don't know if I'll be able."

All the Atlanta area kids arrived on the weekend to celebrate Wheng's birthday. Martin video-taped everyone's individual greeting to our unborn grandson. The hidden purpose in the exercise, of course, was so that Judy could leave him a message from the grandmother he would never know personally. He hadn't yet been named but Judy's message to Mitchell was this: "You belong to all of us. I have been praying for you for months before you were born."

Sunday was a glorious day. Wendi and Abigail had come up to see us. While Wendi saw to Judy I took Abigail with me to see her grandmother. She enjoyed seeing and talking with Abigail but I inadvertently upset my mother when I mentioned the flowers she had been watering weekly were artificial!

Jason had also arrived while we were gone. He brought his mother a beautiful pink rose clipped from his yard. Judy loved it, commenting that it had such a fine fragrance. The boys and Wendi were in rare form all afternoon and entertained Judy mightily. She was awake for the entire time and the pictures we have of that day betray her exuberance.

That night I got the most restful sleep I had had in a long time, getting up to attend to Judy only three times instead of the usual four to five. It was only much later that I soberly realized–after talking with Kevin–that some of Judy's systems had begun to shut down, thus they didn't require as much from her body. Oh, Lord, I don't know how I could have slept those few nights with such knowledge.

During the last time I had gotten up with her that night she had to turn around in order to position herself on the bedside commode. I got myself tangled up in her oxygen lines and she fell a very short distance onto the padded commode as I barely saved my own fall. We were both able to laugh about that as I said, "Well, sweetheart, although we fell in love with each other a long time ago this is the first time we have almost fallen into a commode together!"

Wendi was going to stay a few more days but Abigail had to go back to school so I took her to the airport. We called a private shuttle for that purpose and en route I asked the driver if he had faith in God. He said, "Yes. I'm a muslim." Then he added, "There are four holy books," and he named those of Islam, Christianity, Judaism, and Buddhism. "It's the same God," he said.

As gently as I could I responded, "I'm sorry, but that isn't true. Christianity's God is a god of love. The Koran does not read like a God who loves, forgives, and promises eternal life through man's repentance."

I thought that would be the end of it but he asked me if I knew what the word "Amen" meant. I said, authoritatively, "Of course.

It's a word thanking God." Sitting in the back seat with me, Abigail poked me and whispered, "Grandpa, I think it means 'God be praised.'" I rephrased my answer and credited Abigail. He said that was his name, Amen. When we got to the airport I gave him a generous tip and said, "May the god of Abraham, Isaac and Jacob bless you."

Abigail asked why I had said what I did and I explained I hoped he might reflect on my use of the name Jacob instead of Ishmael, Isaac's other son and the true progenitor of the Islamic world.

NEARER THY GOD

Very early on the morning of September 20, only three days before Judy would be called home, she asked for some morphine for both pain and shortness of breath. I easily administered that and then sat with her for half an hour, rubbing her hands and legs. After a while she looked at me and said in a weak but loving voice, "My comfort."

Wendi was still staying with us and Martin took off another day to be at the house with us. Wendi and I took to our church eleven bags of Judy's clothing for Hurricane Katrina victims. Wendi had somehow managed to go through Judy's clothes at her mother's request, sorting, sizing, and labeling the bags. Those who have lost—or have been on the brink of losing—a loved one understand how difficult it is to see, touch, and smell the clothes of the beloved at such a time and for such a purpose.

I took Wendi to the cemetery to show her how I had updated our cremation bench to reference all three kids' names. I don't have to comment further as to how difficult that moment was. At 11:00 that evening Judy called to me from her sleep-chair in the living room-turned-bedroom. She said, "Call everyone to come. I'm tired. I'm in pain. And I don't want to fight any more." I promised to do so the next day.

An hour later she woke me again. That time she said something that took me by surprise: "Terry, I want to be catheterized. I don't want to struggle with going to the bathroom any more." Frankly, I didn't know how to take her request. At first I thought she might not be rational. I tried to comfort her and told we would talk about it in the morning, but she shook her head, insistent. I didn't argue, but simply changed her wet neck and chest towels and helped her get back to sleep.

At 3:45 A.M. I heard the sound of oxygen escaping through her cannula. Instinctively, I knew that meant her nosepiece was not in place. I gently replaced it only to have her repeat her earlier request, this time being even more specific by saying, "Call Sandy to have me catheterized. I don't want to have to fight going to the bathroom." That time I said, sadly, "Okay, sweetheart," and asked her if she needed some more morphine. She said, "Yes." We again went back to sleep.

At 6:00 A.M. she once again called me awake. This time she not only stated emphatically that she wanted to be catheterized, but right away. I told her it was still too early to call Sandy but I would do so in a little while. That did not suit her and she was insistent I do so immediately. At that point I quit trying to decide what was best for her and exercised her request by placing a call to the hospice group.

Sandy called back within five minutes. She said there was a mandatory patient-update hospice meeting she had to attend until 12 Noon, but if I waited until between 10:00 and 10:30 A.M. and called again, stating it was an emergency, she could probably break away. I told Judy all of that and complied per Sandy's plan. It was the best I could do, but I clearly knew Judy was not only fully rational but committed to her decision.

Before long the medical supply company which had been seeing to our needs arrived with the hospital bed Sandy had ordered. Within minutes of his having set up the bed Sandy arrived and explained to everyone exactly what she was going to do. Then she went about her business. I was stressed to watch, partly because of the difficulty of the catheterization itself, but mostly due to its implication. The date was September 21.

Once catheterized, Judy would not let Wendi and me help her to the commode. We insisted, however, and she reluctantly relented. I was under the mistaken impression that she must surely have to have a bowel movement. As I mentioned earlier I did not understand that her systems had begun to shut down and given that she had not been eating anything the need was simply not there. Judy intuitively knew she had no need, but I didn't, just as I had not understood her motivation for being catheterized.

She then asked for her necklace with the cross and also reminded me of her earlier request to have the cross placed in the cremation urn along with her ashes. I prayed aloud for Judy's comfort and for my strength and added for the first time, "Lord, if it is your will, take her from her suffering."

FINAL DAY

Shortly after I arose on the morning of September 22, 2005 I assessed the night that had just passed. I realized that I could no longer personally provide Judy with the care she needed. I wasn't even able to shift her higher up on the bed from where she had slumped during the night. I knew it was time for in-patient hospice. I again called nurse Sandy and she said she would make it happen. In subsequent telephone conversations with both Wendi and Martin I received their blessings. Jason was out of cell phone reach.

As for my dear Judy, I told her of the decision and added that there was a good chance they would honor her number one request at that time, which was to be able to sit up on her bed and dangle her feet over the side. That was all the incentive she needed to assent.

Within an hour or so a certified nurse's assistant came to get her physically prepared for the transfer. Then Sandy arrived to take care of admission details as well as see to Judy's emotional state. Judy's only comment was that she thought she was finished with the Lord's work for her on this earth. She qualified that by saying she believed all of her children and their spouses believed in Jesus Christ as their Lord and Savior, but added, "He must yet have something for me to do since I'm still here."

Sandy handled things perfectly. She said, " Judy, that 'someone' might be me as I have some issues in life that your incredible testimony has already addressed." To this she added, "And the Lord may have a job for you in heaven that isn't yet quite in order. When He's ready, He'll call for you."

Judy's youngest sister, Rusti, called to update us on their father, who was improving in ICU. Then Rusti turned to the unimaginable task of saying goodbye to her loving sister. I could barely manage listening to the conversation. Judy had already had that conversation with both our daughter and granddaughter.

The in-patient hospice people arrived an hour early. As they put her on the stretcher and carried her out to the ambulance I walked alongside her and held her hand, right up until the moment they hoisted her aboard. I will never forget her expression. It seemed to reflect resignation tempered with anticipation. I quickly gathered up a few things and jumped into my car to follow.

Within forty-five minutes we arrived at Haven House. No sooner had we gotten her into a room than I made known Judy's request to sit up and dangle her feet over the side of the bed. They responded instantly in the affirmative and took the appropriate action. Judy was so happy over that simple situation that she perked up measurably.

Martin arrived shortly after that, then Jason and Wheng. While Jason and Wheng talked with her, Martin and I ran to a grocery store to pick up a non-spill drinking cup (which I again incorrectly perceived to be a need; she had no further need of water). Neither Martin nor I had eaten so we grabbed a quick sandwich for ourselves. The trip was really more of an excuse for Martin and me to talk. He was quite concerned for me, and I for him. We talked through the sandwiches and tears.

It seems such a simple thing, but Judy was so delighted to have the freedom of sitting up, as she had for most of the nineteen months following her diagnosis, but which she had so sorely missed for the previous two days. She actually held court for nearly four hours. Though weak, she was quite responsive and complained of no pain. As always, she simply enjoyed having family gathered around. She smiled, she listened, she even interacted. She reiterated for every one there the same two things she had said on several occasions over the previous few days about her family and her work on earth being done. My gentle Judy was ready and prepared for the Lord to call her home.

That evening she spoke a few words which I thought were strange. I had never before heard them from her. She said, "God makes it so easy to cross over. He just asks if you want to go to sleep." What are we to make of that? Was she so close to her appointed time that in her sleep she had had a vision or a dream from God that He was about to call her home?

At about midnight she complained of having difficulty breathing. I called the nurse and between us we carefully checked out her oxygen line and administered a small dose of liquid Morphine. That was, in fact, the only Morphine she had asked for over the previous twenty-four hours. I looked lovingly into her face and wiped away my tears. I kissed her ever so gently before crawling back onto my cot, which was next to her bed. I was both exhausted and inconsolable.

At 6:00 A.M. I awoke to check on her. Her breathing was extremely shallow. Gently, I again kissed her. This time it was in the form of three tender little kisses to her forehead. She used to refer to such as her "butterfly kisses," because of my moustache. As I did this she softly said her last words, "I want to sleep."

God granted her last wish as He called her home at 8:30 A.M. on September 23, 2005. Unspeakably grieved as I was, I yet knew—as Bernie Siegel wrote in *Love, Medicine and Miracles*, "Death is not a failure. Not choosing to take on the challenge of life is." Judy not only loved the challenge to the very end of her life on this earth, she served her Lord and Savior to the fullest. In retrospect I was tempted to second guess myself in not having prayed more with her in those final hours, holding her hand or perhaps even whispering in her ear. I came to the realization, however, that that would have only been to my benefit, not hers. There is nothing I could have said to God that would have spoken more eloquently for her than the life she lived.

Part II: Journeying Alone

LIFE AHEAD

At 9:00 on the evening following Judy's passing I wrote the following in my journal: "This has been the single most painful day of my life. I am hurting emotionally as I never knew a human could. Better than ever I think I understand a little of God the Father's pain in losing His only begotten Son. And as much as I loved Judy He yet loved her more."

That God loved her so is not only the ultimate consolation for me, His love belongs to every single person alive. And it is He to whom anyone can turn in their time of either greatest need or finest praise.

Twice that morning I had already knelt, weeping, before God to talk to Him about Judy, both praising Him for healing her and asking the same for myself. During the night that had just passed I had a fleeting thought that given the option to stay here on earth or join Judy in the presence of God I would opt for the latter. That was the only time in my life I have ever found myself truly in a state of depression, but I knew that it was not chronic. Instinctively, I knew it was situational and that I would recover.

On the Sunday afternoon following the Friday of Judy's passing all four of my Atlanta area kids joined me in cleaning up the house. That was so helpful for me not to be alone. Mike Roper arrived shortly afterwards and we talked for about an hour concerning funeral arrangements. He also circled up the five of us and prayerfully thanked God for Judy in all of our lives.

I wasn't much help in the cleaning effort as all I could manage was to wander around the house. When Betty and Wheng fixed all of us a special meal that night I told them that Judy would have been so happy merely to see them using her new oven range. It had been some time since Judy was no longer able to stand and cook, and I had resorted to using the microwave exclusively.

A dozen or so prayer requests had come in for Judy's attention during the final two days of her life on this earth and I took it upon myself to pray for them individually–as Judy always had–and then prayed one last time for all of those in her five accumulated prayer notebooks. They dated back several years prior to her diagnosis.

For you who have experienced one or more of life's toughest lessons, take heart through these special words of prayer and thankfulness: Father in heaven, we become confused in the darkness of what we don't understand. Help us to see that the grace You have shown us time and again is only a taste of Your ability to use all eternity to surprise us over and over with Your goodness.

SUNDAY'S NEW DAY

As I was preparing to go to church on Sunday Martin called to check on me. I could instantly detect the sadness in his voice–both for the loss of the mother he so loved–and for me. The moment spoke to me. While I was neither angry with God nor complaining, I had nevertheless whined to Him a great deal over the previous several days. I resolved, with the Lord's help, to take hold of myself.

At church, people came up to me and hugged and loved on me. Quite deliberately I sat in the third pew center row–where Judy and I often sat—determined to make my first post-Judy service up close and personal. Within a minute or two of the start of the service one of the Men of the Way members and his wife spotted me from across the sanctuary and came to sit with me. Near the end of the service I got up to attend one of the oil-anointing stations. A fellow Stephen Minister blessed me as I knelt at the altar in praise of God. Then, the couple sitting with me came up and further comforted me by joining me in private prayer.

Something else took place that Sunday–unbeknownst to me at the time—but which would have life-changing ramifications for me over the weeks and months to come. Yet another Stephen Minister–one whom I did not know and would not meet for several more weeks—attended that same service. As she sat by herself some pews behind me she recognized me from a mutual friend's comments. Her thought was, "Poor man. He just lost his wife." She had by no means fully recovered from the one-year trauma in her own life.

As a person nears the autumn of his or her life it is much easier to not only contemplate one's mortality, but also to realize that the material accumulation of that life will soon be as nothing. One such man died and upon his death a close friend inquired, "How much did he leave behind?" To that another friend answered, "All of it." There is a serious perspective on that humorous note. Scripture teaches that we *can* make deposits to our heavenly account before we die. In Philippians 4:17 the apostle Paul refers to heavenly treasures as "what may be credited to your account."

Wendi told me she would like to speak at her mother's funeral service. I asked our son-in-law to do so as well. In particular I asked him to make a connection between God's love for us all and His covenant of marriage between man and woman. He said being asked to speak at Judy's funeral was the greatest honor ever accorded him.

SYMPHONY RE-VISITED

On Saturday, October 1 we began the final step of the dance to which Judy and I had first been called 48 years earlier. That first date, mentioned earlier in this story, had been the high school post-football game dance. The time had come for me to deliver Judy's eulogy. How is it that–within the space of a few sentences–my life rushes from Judy's and my first date to her eulogy?

I spoke publicly about the first love of my life, the mother of our three children, and someone who I believe positively influenced everyone who ever crossed her path. It was the single greatest honor of my 67 years. In the words of William Booth–the founder of the Salvation Army, at the time he lost his wife–"There has been taken from me the delight of my eyes and the inspiration of my soul."

When I told a friend on the phone a few days before the planned celebration of Judy's life that I was going to deliver the eulogy, he said, "How are you going to manage that?" On my own, I said I couldn't, but Almighty God would not only get me through that, He will get me through the rest of my life.

The main thing I tried to accomplish in the eulogy was to accurately describe Judy. That effort was best done through two sentences in particular. They were these: "Judy *showed* us her witness, rather than simply *telling* us. Her life was *real* and it was lived for her Lord and Savior."

I commented during the eulogy that upon spotting her for the first time in 1956 in the high school halls of my junior year, I was struck dumb by her beauty. To that I added that one of my good

Christian friends humorously said to me, "How long could that have taken?"

When asked at the video testimonial she made for our church only eight days before her passing about the greatest blessing in her life outside of her salvation through Christ, she said simply, "My family." She was referring to our three children, our three in-law children and our three grandchildren, even though the third grandchild had not yet been born. We both believed a child is a human being at conception, not birth. The womb is merely our incubus until we are able to be sustained outside of that protective environment.

The service's beautiful lyrics and vocal solo of *Safely Home*, sung by a wonderfully talented friend were due to the efforts of our church's former minister of music, who also played the accompaniment. Both the hymn and its rendition still speak hauntingly and strongly to me.

I closed my eulogy by reiterating that while I still wept and wailed over my loss, yet did I have joy in my heart for Judy's gain, for she was not only healed, she was home. Because of the promise of salvation through Christ Jesus, Judy will enjoy everlasting life in the presence of God. And because of His God-breathed promise to us in holy Scripture she will be bodily resurrected at the second coming of the Savior of the world.

RE-GATHERING

Mine wasn't the only tribute delivered at the service. Wendi did a wonderful job in both humorously and reverently characterizing her mother. Mike Roper, the same pastor who had helped guide me through parts of my Stephen Ministry training and who prayed with and served home communion to Judy and me on many occasions, had not only officiated at the repeating of our vows but then handled the funeral service as well. As a reference to Mike's connection to Judy and to our family, the senior service director at the funeral home said to me following the service, "She must have been an exceptional woman. I've known Mike for many years and have seen him conduct many, many services, but this is the first time I thought he might lose his composure, especially when I saw his lips quiver." At that very point he said Mike had looked upward, obviously turning to the Lord for strength.

Ironically, Mike has also been instrumental in two other areas of my life. He not only helped Helga through her counseling long prior to our ever having met, but he also performed *our* wedding ceremony in 2006!

A very special friend to both Helga and me and also both a fellow Stephen Minister and Stephen Ministry leader—as well as someone who has suffered more of life's toughest lessons than anyone I know—shared something special with Wendi the day before the funeral. She said that her mother was the most Godly woman she had ever met.

As for Kevin's message, he did an incredible job of bringing everything to closure in the Lord's desire to save each and every one of us from His righteous wrath at a fallen mankind. He gave the precise formula to those who might be thinking about their situation in that regard. Did it touch anyone's heart who hadn't yet surrendered to Him? I don't know the answer to that, but a good friend of mine—and the self-described agnostic whom I mentioned earlier in the story—said to me after the service: "That was the most awesome funeral service I have ever attended."

I recently read something in the waiting room of my dentist that has stayed with me, both in my mind and on the desk in my office. It speaks to me about the comparison between Judy (as well as all of those who are saved through acceptance of the free gift of God's grace) and those who have never come to grips with their mortality and separation from God. The sentence is this: "Unable are the saved to die, for faith in Him yields immortality." Who wouldn't want such a guarantee, if only its meaning is pondered?

Judy was surely commended by God upon her entrance to heaven simply because she sought first to honor Him. She had faith like Noah–to whom God said, "It's going to rain, Son. Build an ark," which required him–who knew it had never before rained upon earth–to live by faith. Judy had no less faith. And by faith alone she was justified by God. You and I–as believers–are also justified in our faith and thus, even though we die, shall we yet live.

As Judy spent her final hours on this earth all of her family and friends were weeping, yet she was smiling. Why? Because she lived a life in Christ and thereby knew that whatever was ahead of her would be in God's presence, for faith does indeed yield immortality.

CHANGE IN CRISES

In the weeks following the crisis of experience came the crisis of remembrance and loss. I was never so grateful for company as when I arrived back home from the cemetery that funeral day to find one of my children there. Jason had already put away all the toys in the basement play room which our grandchildren had enthusiastically left behind. Then we sat down together to animatedly watch the Atlanta Falcons uncharacteristically win–that season, anyway—a football game.

Later, as I sat in the room which had been Judy's and my family room for 26 years, I knew I would grieve deeply. I also realized one other thing. This was, nevertheless, the beginning of the rest of my life without what had been the love of my life. As such, it was also time to end my "journal of our journey," which I had begun more than nineteen months earlier. That evening I sat at my computer and composed a list of things I believed would make me happy in my new life.

Here is that entry, dated October 3, 2005, ten days after Judy's passing:

God gives us the ability to choose how we feel. I will greatly mourn her loss, but I will also honor her memory by choosing to be happy. What are the things that would both make me happy and honor her?

1. Take great joy in the Lord, be obedient, and seek to glorify Him in everything I do.
2. Allow my church, my friends, and especially my family, to love and help me; and in turn give more of myself to each of them.
3. Maintain and perhaps expand my newsletter ministry, the sole purpose for which now (with Judy's passing), would be to glorify Him through spreading the gospel.
4. Downsize my household goods and belongings, giving what I can to help others.
5. Write a fourth book; this one to be based on the lessons learned through Judy's and my journey.
6. With time, ask the Lord to bring a loving and godly woman into my life–perhaps one who has also lost a spouse or experienced some other traumatic event in her own life–but someone with whom I could share, through marriage, both life and love.

   (Note: I did not know at the time I wrote this that Judy had shared with her hospice nurse, Sandy, that she had prayed I would find a new wife. I have no doubt, however, that she would have qualified her prayer by asking God to pick that woman for me. He certainly did answer Judy's, mine, and Helga's prayers).
7. Try not to be worrisome and obsessed over my tremendous loss in Judy, for she–the symphony of my life–was the most joyful and happiest person I have ever known. God willing, I will meet another.

I will both pray and trust in Him for His will in these regards. I am father, grandfather, and widower, but first I am a man of faith and of God, dependent upon Christ, my Lord and Savior.

GOD CLOSES ONE DOOR/ OPENS ANOTHER

I believe the following—which some wonderfully enlightened but anonymous soul has written–to be true: " What we all need is enough happiness to make us sweet, enough trials to make us strong, enough sorrow to keep us human, and enough hope to make us happy."

I think I tended to believe my loss was greater than my children's. Theirs was certainly just as great to them. When a loved one dies, our emotions cross the line from loss and sorrow to something far more intense and lasting. That something is grief. The closer we were to that person the more intense the grief. One thing I feel certain about is that Judy would not have wanted me to deeply mourn her indefinitely. One day I will see her again and confirm that very point.

Jesus knew what it meant to grieve for the loss of a loved one. When His friend Lazarus died and Jesus came to his tomb, His grief was not hidden: "Jesus wept" (John 11:35). When I grieve over Judy I am not sorrowing for her, but for me. When you or I grieve over someone who has died in Christ, our grief isn't a sign of weak faith, but of great love.

I read all of the insightful brochures the hospice group continued to send me, deriving much help and comfort from them. One of the greatest truths I learned and accepted was that while death ends a physical presence it doesn't end a relationship. At first I didn't understand that. After a while I came to appreciate that I could create a new relationship with Judy–one of heart, mind and spirit, incorporating her values and passions into my own life. Wow, what a lesson that was and is. As a result of that awareness I decided to continue my written ministry as the New Day Newsletter.

As I came to grips with actually ending the odyssey of our wonderful journey together I closed it with a final letter written to her the evening of October 7.

Dear Judy,

It has now been two weeks since you crossed over to be in God's presence, healed from your suffering of more than a year and a half after your diagnosis. I am struggling mightily, alternating between knowing the joy you must have to be in His presence, and wallowing in self-pity over my loss.

When I look at pictures of you, you become more beautiful and precious to me than I can bear. It is delight born of grief that I recall what we talked about over and over again during those nineteen months–that we had been incredibly blessed with so many years to laugh, cry and share with one another.

My joy during your illness was to care for you in every way possible. I loved every minute of that time. Even when you suffered the most you offered so much to me and to our children and to our friends, even to strangers. I now close this journal of our journey together, sweetheart. I will see you again in an instant.

Part III: A New Journey

A NEW DAY

The Bible tells us that we should seek qualified counseling in making decisions. First, we should seek God's counsel; then, if we are married, the counsel of our spouse; following that, the counsel of our living parents; and beyond that, the counsel of other Christians.

I first sought the counsel of Judy's own Stephen Minister concerning disposition of Gracie. I had wanted to donate her little-used power scooter to our Jacksonville kids' congregation, but getting it down there in a timely fashion was problematic. I wanted that neat little scooter–which had become for me a difficult visual reminder of things—out of my garage and into use for someone. Valorie suggested the Roswell Nursing Home so I took her counsel and donated Gracie in Judy's name.

I also asked Valorie about some professional Christian counseling for myself and she made arrangements for me to contact the director at Mt. Pisgah's The Summit. I looked forward to beginning those sessions as soon as I returned from a planned trip to Iowa for closure with all of Judy's family.

Counsel is so important for healing purposes. And although healing comes slowly it does come if one trusts in the Lord. Consider the notion of counsel in the biblical Job's case. His suffering was so intense that one day he found himself sitting on a dung heap, cursing the day he was born, and crying out in relentless pain. His suffering was so great that his wife–bless her untrusting soul–even counseled Job to curse God, that he might die and be relieved of his agony. He heeded neither his wife's advice nor that of his shallow friends.

LIFE'S TOUGHEST LESSONS

He did, however, make a mistake in questioning God directly. For His own reasons God apparently found that interesting and plied Job with a few questions of his own, beginning with a simple one: "Where were you when I laid the foundations of the universe?" In effect, God answered Job with Himself. My point here is that the answer Job ultimately came to realize is that his hope in the midst of his incredible suffering rested with God. To whom else could we turn in our most desperate moments?

I did not make a single entry in my journal for the two-week period in mid-October of 2005 as I trekked to Iowa to close things out with Judy's sisters and their families. I also took time to visit with Judy's best friend since their school days of orchestra, mixed chorus, and double dating. I stayed at the home of my own best friend of nearly fifty years. Together, Jack and I not only viewed the video celebration of Judy's life as we reminisced, cried and prayed, but we pitched many games of horseshoes. He loved to tell the story of how he once "saved Judy's life" by chasing off an habitual third grade schoolyard tormentor of hers. He wasn't exaggerating as Judy was always quick to remember the story as well.

At the assisted living home where Judy's father lived I gathered with her two sisters and their families to view the funeral service CD. This would be the final time I was to view the CD until more than a year later. The sisters held each other as they sobbed during parts of the recorded service. Later, we all enjoyed a steak and fresh catfish dinner for the entire family as we sat outside in the cool October air in front of a crackling wood fire. Only two years prior to that Judy has been happily with me in a precursor to that same family venue.

As I prepared to make the thirty-mile gravel-and-asphalt drive from the Postma's home to Jack's house, Judy's middle sister surprised me by walking me to a four-candle memorial she had lit in their backyard. She asked me to pray for her and for her family. I was grateful for such a first-time request from her and asked God to draw each of them closer to Him.

I paid one last visit to Judy's father, who would pass away six months later at age 89. He was still remarkably in charge of his faculties and he shared with me a profound comment. When his grandfather lay on his death bed Judy's father asked him why he had to die. The grandfather answered, "The old must and the young may."

COMING TO GRIPS

Within a few days of the one-month anniversary of Judy's crossing over I made my first visit to grief counseling. The most telling moment in that session came when Counselor David asked me about the most negative image I had of Judy's passing. I tearfully described two of them for him. He asked me to close my eyes and think of those two images. Then, he prayed for God to replace those images for me with something positive. No sooner had he said that than up popped an image of Judy's face. She had the most incredibly beautiful and radiant smile and she was smiling down on me. I clearly remember saying to David–no, I actually shouted—"He did it! Praise the Lord." I never again had to deal with either of those negative images.

I wrote a final letter to Judy. Here are excerpts:

> Dear Judy, as I sit here tonight listening to our/my music barely more than four weeks since you crossed over to be with our Lord and Savior, I cannot keep from wailing and crying over my loss. Several times, in desperation, I have reached out for Jesus' hand, as you so often did during the times you felt tested by procedures, anxiety, or pain. He calmed me as He always did you, but I still carry incredible sadness close to my heart.
>
> My tears cannot be for you, however, since you left behind a burdensome body and found reward with your coronation. I don't know whether or not this will be my final letter to you, but I long to say this one more time: I have

always loved you. Oddly, I know this to be true more desperately since your passing. My hope is to be able to honor you through the rest of my life on this earth, even if I should some day find another to love and with whom to share the remainder of this life. Your Terry.

FULL CIRCLE

A few weeks after having written the above letter I drove to Jacksonville, Florida for an eight-day trip to see KWAK. I drove most of the way down in tears as I played Judy's and my favorite music. I spent a part of the first three mornings in conversation and sharing with Wendi after we got Kevin off to work and Abigail and Karsten off to school. I really unloaded, even telling her of my desire to–with Judy's prior blessing–find a Godly woman as my new helper in life. She fully understood, for which I was very grateful. A few days into the visit came the evening's conversation which began this book.

Only a few days into my return to Atlanta my HVAC crashed and the Lord interestingly used that event to my growth and to His glory. A service tech required several trips over a two-day period to fix my furnace problems. I shared my tragedy with him because he knew Judy and me from previous visits over the years. He had some questions for me. He was concerned about his relationships with his new family, as well as with his self-admitted declining prayer life. I talked to him and prayed with him, asking God to draw him closer. We concluded our time together with my giving him a Bible and strongly suggesting that he and his wife find a church.

Ironically, some months later he came to my new house twenty miles away to install an additional HVAC system in my new bride's and my newly finished basement. He and I picked up where we had left off months earlier. My, how God does work with us!

CHANGING LANES

In searching my mega-church's announcements' bulletin and listing of various small group meetings and the many Sunday School classes, I noticed one curiously labeled as "Singles ACTS." At first glance I thought it must be a reference to a study of the Book of Acts, but upon further reading I was surprised to learn the name was an acronym standing for Adults Called To Service. I was intrigued to discover the group was actually a singles Bible study class.

I decided to give it a try after receiving a recommendation by my former Stephen Ministry care giver. The class teacher was the same person who wrote the forward to this book. In addition to Wayne and his wife, Nancy, there were about thirty singles present, representing ages from perhaps forty to seventy.

I arrived at the classroom early and within minutes Wayne asked me if I knew the only other person in the room at the moment. He was referring to someone I had already—but very briefly—met the week before at a Stephen Ministry meeting. In fact, I had politely introduced myself to her at the time. She had rejoined both Mt. Pisgah and the Stephen Ministry group during the time I had been traveling to Iowa and Florida after about a two-year intervening period when she had belonged to another church.

I was immediately struck by both her beauty and her carriage. This was a woman who obviously combined self-confidence with faith. I deliberately positioned myself directly across from her in the classroom's U-shaped table configuration. The study of Luke got underway for the others, but my mind began racing with improbable thoughts not connected with the book of Luke. That went like this:

"She's beautiful. Is she available? She must be. She's in a singles class, isn't she? And she's a Stephen Minister in the bargain! Pay attention to Wayne and the lesson. Phooey. I'm watching Helga. Dear Lord, could this be the woman you're sending to be my new helper? Now, that's ridiculous. I've only met her twice for a total of two minutes and exchanged with her barely that many words."

Suddenly, I heard Wayne saying they had a newcomer with them today. Did I want to introduce myself? I would. And did. I also commented on being privileged to find this group now that I had lost my wife to cancer five weeks earlier after having cared for her for nineteen months during her illness.

As the hour wore on I came to the decision that I was going to invite this beautiful German-American woman to have lunch with me. Again, my thoughts were running rampant. "When would I ask her? The very next day, that's when. Of course, at Monday night's Stephen Ministry meeting. Lord, how do I go about doing that? It's been 46 years since I last asked someone who wasn't my wife for a date. Oh, and one other huge thing. She looks to be on the borderline of being too young for me. What to do? I'll sort that out at home. What's that Wayne is saying? Oh. Both the hour and the lesson are over. He wants to know who's going to pray us out. I can do that."

I barely slept that night, pondering so many questions concerning someone with whom I had yet to have a conversation. I think I prayed about that. I hope I did, but I don't remember. I knew one thing for certain, however. I needed some direct input. Who was this woman whom it seemed the Lord had put directly in front of me with a sign over her head reading, "She's right here, my son!"

Early the next morning I phoned the one person I was certain knew both of us—Valorie. I nonchalantly asked if she had a few minutes to talk, and if so, could I come to her office for that purpose . . . right away!

She did. I rushed over to the church, but then beat around the bush with several extraneous questions before getting to the point of my call. I led up to it by saying I valued her opinion, both as a friend and as a spiritual leader and wanted her "take" on something. I could see her gird herself ever so subtly, as if I might be wanting to talk about a problem I had with Stephen Ministry, the church, or perhaps with God! I am absolutely certain she must have thought it was something serious. I took a deep breath and blurted out my question as if it were one word, "I'm-thinking-of-asking-Helga-to-have-a-cup-of-coffee-with-me-what-do-you-think?"

At first she didn't even respond. I think she had to download the input. Then she had a look about her that said, "That's *it*? I thought you were going to unload something heavy on me." After a few seconds she regained her composure and said, much to my relief, "You know, I think she might be ready for that. It's been a year since her husband left her."

We discussed things for a few more minutes and then Valorie took stock of the situation before handing me back my words, with some added qualification. "I understand that after such a difficult nineteen months of caring for Judy and then some time of not having that same relationship, you need to talk with a woman again." Boy, for such a slow starter she caught on quickly! After that, she allayed my fear about the difference in our ages not fitting within my parameters.

That same evening at Stephen Ministry I was fully prepared to ask Helga to have lunch with me the following Sunday. I had rehearsed Plan A many times during that day. I had it nailed. I arrived quite early, but it didn't take long for me to realize Plan A would not work. Helga was a no show! She was taking care of her two grandsons that evening.

Before I left the class that night I had worked out Plan B. It would be an e-mail invitation which I would send to her at work come daybreak. Early the next day, according to plan, I e-mailed her with my invitation. I concluded the note by suggesting she check me out with the two female Stephen Ministry leaders I knew who would give me at least a C+. I tried to set a light tone by stating that it had been years since I last "served any time."

Two hours later I received her e-mailed reply. It was in the affirmative! And, to my surprise and delight, she even mentioned that she planed to attend the Singles Class Thanksgiving Day dinner the evening before our Sunday luncheon and, if I planned to attend, perhaps "we could talk a bit there." I figured she was thinking that would give her an out for the following day's lunch in the event she pegged me as a doofus.

I spent the remainder of the day bouncing around on air from one errand and task to another. When I went to my counseling session and shared my news I asked the counselor if I was premature in terms of seeing someone so soon. David responded with something I would never have considered. He told me that I had not been grieving for merely the period of time that had elapsed following Judy's passing, but that my journey in that respect had actually begun when she had first been diagnosed. His rationale had to do with the reality that Judy's and my relationship had begun to change at that point, simply because of the increasing limitations imposed upon us by her illness.

HOW NOT TO BEGIN
A RELATIONSHIP

Saturday came and for one of the few times in my life I shaved twice in the same day. I arrived early at the class's Thanksgiving dinner, but within minutes of my arrival Helga swept in, wearing a long black coat and carrying a covered dish. I immediately followed her into the kitchen, barely allowing her to put down her dish before engaging her in conversation. In that process I said, "I've reserved two chairs for us at one of the tables in the dining room," hoping she wouldn't respond with something like, "Whatever."

As she prepared to leave at the evening's end she mentioned that she was going to the early church service the next morning. I said I was also. Then she said the magic words: "We'll sit together." When I got home I pumped my fist and shouted to an empty house, "All right! I have a half-day Sunday date!"

What an incredible day was that! I sat next to this fine-looking woman with medium–almost golden–blond hair, eyes bluer than my own and a wit to match mine. After church we went to my car where I gave her the single salmon-colored rose I had purchased for her earlier that morning. I didn't know I had also chosen one of her favorite colors! We sat together during the Sunday School class before going to lunch at Café Au Lait. At the restaurant I was nervous, afraid I wouldn't make a good impression. Worse, that I might say something I shouldn't. On the latter count I was prophetic.

I had arranged with the Korean owner a special table and service by him personally. He had known Judy, as it was the same restaurant at which we had spent our Valentine's lunch after her tentative diagnosis in the pulmonologist's office. He seemed happy I had chosen his restaurant for the first meeting with my new lady friend.

Helga and I talked for an hour and a half. She first shared her story with me, being quite transparent in that respect. She also told me she had been to a divorce recovery retreat only the week before and was feeling wrung out at that time. She even shared that she had actually prayed for someone to come into her life one day before she received my e-mail asking her to lunch. I could hardly believe what I was hearing. She was also quite candid in sharing that immediately following receipt of my e-mail she called a close friend to talk with her about her anxieties over the invitation.

Helga finished sharing and I took my turn. I told her something of Judy's and my wonderful life together as well as my Christian witness. I also shared that because I had enjoyed such a wonderful marriage I, too, had prayed about finding someone. Then, I nearly blew myself out of the water. How do I know? Because my next sentence caused her to raise the flat of her hand and say, "Whoa!"

Hey, all I said was, "I'm looking to find a Godly woman I can court and marry." To Helga's credit she didn't immediately jump up and dash for the nearest exit. Instead, she opted to indulge me for a little longer. She did cue me in on something, however, by responding to my comment with , "Look, I'm not ready for anything more than event dating."

Both resilient and resourceful, I immediately shifted gears and went to Plan C. I assured her that "event dating" (a term which I had never before heard) was exactly what I had in mind.

Though we were each walking strongly with the Lord at the time, both of us had truly come to Christ late in life. Within only a few weeks' time both of us would also come to feel the Lord had drawn us together, saying in effect, "Well done, good and faithful servant. Here is your new helper."

That night I read from some more of the grief materials Judy's hospice organization continued to provide for me. One paragraph practically reached out and grabbed me by my throat. It read: "You can either believe 'I will never love or be happy again,' or 'It's possible I will find love and happiness in the future.' Whatever beliefs we create for ourselves, we will set about gathering evidence to support them."

I must have re-read that paragraph half a dozen times. Wow! I thanked God once again for all the blessings as well as the trials in my life. We simply cannot thank Him for the one and omit the other and yet claim to place our complete trust in Him.

HELGA'S GENESIS

Helga Sens was born in Cuxhaven, Germany during the Winter of 1951. Cuxhaven is a beautiful city of some 100,000 people located directly on the North Sea in the very northwestern corner of Germany. In 1963 Helga's family moved forty or so miles south to Bremerhaven where she finished three years of secretarial study following the standard German schooling format of tenth grade. As a young girl she was feisty, not one to let a dare or challenge rest, including attempted bullying by boys. Those unlucky boys usually regretted having picked on her and rarely tried it a second time.

As with most Germans, Helga attended confirmation classes at her Lutheran church and was confirmed at age 15. Unfortunately, that was hardly the beginning of a relationship with the Lord. Rather, it was the end of attending church. That was the standard in her culture, both then and now. Once confirmed, most Germans (and Europeans in general) consider themselves finished with religion and the need to open the Bible, much less pray, study the Word, and seek God's will for themselves. As an aside, when she and I visited her German hometown some months after our marriage I asked one of her 40-something family members if she owned a Bible. Her response was to say, "Of course." When I asked if she read from it, she again responded with, "Of course." She qualified her answer, however, with, "but not since confirmation."

The young Helga was a go-getter from an early age and she honed her school-taught English by baby-sitting with American soldier families' children. She understood very clearly how to capitalize on the four-to-one American-dollar-to-German mark currency advantage and thus earned good money for herself. It was hardly any wonder she wanted to study banking, but her parents insisted she learn secretarial skills.

Helga would be dealt difficult hands for much of her life. And while it was her nature to persevere, she was not blessed with a seeker's heart early in life, even in times of major stress. At age 24 she was stricken with rheumatoid arthritis in her hands, wrists, knees, feet, and most of her body joints. The affliction and its pain continued to worsen. After four years of trying every available medication—without success—she could barely walk. Finding herself having to hold onto office rails and walls in order to get around, her body was calling for a wheelchair while doctors said her last resort would be injections.

Through all of this she, nevertheless, willed herself to work hard, both at home and on her job with a German-owned company in the Atlanta area. One day, she forgot to take her medication. Having forgotten once she didn't bother taking her meds for several more days. She was suddenly amazed to realize she didn't seem to need the medicine. She stopped taking it altogether.

Before long, and through God's grace, she recovered completely. Helga would give Him no due, however, for she did not know Him. And one side effect of the illness remained, perhaps a different aspect of her ongoing pruning. During the course of her illness her personality changed from merely having a strong will to becoming mean and hostile to others. She would suffer much more pruning before she would turn to Him in search of true meaning in her life.

MISFORTUNE IN MARRIAGE

While only 18-years old Helga met and married an American soldier stationed in Bremerhaven and returned with him to the United States to make their home in the Atlanta area. Out of that marriage came her only child, a daughter, Tracie. Sadly, after 13 years of trying hard to make the combination of a musician's night life and a translator-secretary's day life work, they could not find common ground. Divorce was the result. Mother raised daughter and later was presented with two grandsons (Tyler and Aaron) born to Tracie and her husband, David. All remained in the greater Atlanta area.

After seven years of a difficult single life, Helga tried marriage again—this time to a man who professed to be a Christian. He not only didn't possess its conviction but he succumbed to infidelity and a marriage-breaking addiction and cover-up. Fifteen years of trying to make an obviously failing marriage work came to an abrupt end when her husband left home. When that marriage ended in divorce, Helga hit rock bottom and found she had no energy to work and little will to accomplish tasks of any kind.

One evening, en route from work, her desperation nearly overcame her. She contemplated running her car at high speed into the next telephone pole. Only the thought of her beloved daughter and her two precious grandsons kept her from doing so. When she got home she went straight to her bedroom and got on her knees, crying out in desperation to God, asking Him to take her enormous pain and heartache away.

HEALING HELGA

Some months later, in a letter of encouragement to a friend struggling with her own divorce, Helga wrote, telling her exactly what had happened to her. In that letter she added that in the morning following her crying out to the Lord the huge knot residing in her stomach had disappeared. In its place she found wonderful thoughts about changes she needed to make in her life. At her weakest point in time the Lord had reached out to her with new strength.

It was at that point that her life began to dramatically change. She would never forget when and where those blessings had begun, that it was through nothing she did. She had finally given up on holding back, and had begun surrendering her life to God.

In an attempt to salvage things in the latter part of her second marriage she took her budding Christianity to a three-day women-only spiritual retreat (Walk to Emmaus), sponsored by a Christian counseling couple. Thinking the Walk was merely a standard weekend retreat that would allow her time to read and reflect, she quickly regretted going.

She later related that had she not been driven to the site by her sponsors she would have bolted for home, thinking she had somehow gotten shanghaied by a cult of some kind! By Saturday morning, however, she had not only recovered from that thought, she placed her baggage and life at the foot of the cross, further surrendering to the Lord Jesus. She would never again be the same woman who had rebelled against the Lord's revealing Himself to her.

With the inevitable divorce from her second husband Helga resolved never to marry again. She would tell herself and others, "I have failed miserably at picking men. I am not going to go looking for another. If the Lord wants me to have another man in my life He will have to place him squarely in front of me."

The road to our actual Sunday School meeting, however, was immediately preceded by yet another weekend retreat for Helga. Perhaps wanting to capture some of the passive time of reflection she hadn't gotten on her Emmaus Walk–yet still wanting to discover how she herself might have done a better job in helping to fashion success in her two failed marriages—she signed up as a single for a spiritual Love and Respect marriage conference, hosted by a local church. She was able to talk two of her best friends (a married couple) into attending with her.

It was a highly emotional experience for Helga. Following the conference she cried the entire trip home, once again calling out to the Lord for help and asking for Him to bring someone into her life who would be her helper. Only eight days later she and I would meet in that fated Sunday School class-room setting.

ROAD TO RECOVERY

As I think back on that very emotional conference experience for Helga, I am amazed that she had both the imagination and desire to try to learn what she might have done differently to hold things together. Most people simply look for reinforcement for the notion that they have done everything right. She felt called to a reexamination of herself through her second marriage, even though she was the one who had been betrayed from the very beginning. As lamentable as the circumstances were, she was being shaped for a purpose.

Often, God does bring calamity into our lives. It is never evil, however, and always has a purpose. The problem we humans have with this is that not only do we rarely understand it—often choosing to question Him—but we seldom seek to learn from it. What little patience we have. The lessons learned from calamity are always in God's time. And unless we are willing to faithfully stay at our posts and listen, we may quickly compound our mistakes.

Lest you, reader, think I dishonored Judy by too quickly appearing to move forward with life, put that thought aside. My loss was–and is today–extremely painful. Happiness is a decision, and I chose to be happy. The one whom I mourn and whose physical body is gone is still alive in me. The same can be said of your lost one. He or she is alive in our memories, in the way he or she shaped who we are–and we will always treasure that presence. By the same token God did not allow any tragic circumstance in our lives for the purpose of breaking a bruised reed or putting out a smoldering wick.

He wants us to recognize our dependance upon Him and He wants us to grow from such pruning.

God not only *knows* what is best for us, He *wants* what is best for us. How do we know? He *loves* us! Hey, if God loves us enough to send His Son into the world to die for us such that we can gain eternal salvation through that relationship, then would He not also want what is *best* for us? Judy would not have wanted me to deeply mourn her indefinitely. Granted that I know little of what is on the other side of death, but I do know one thing. I know God was there to greet Judy, and He will be there to greet you and I as believers as well. It is not an easy road, but it is certain, if we cast our lot with Him.

ODE TO SPIRITUAL INTIMACY

Thanksgiving of 2005 was brought to me by my Atlanta area sons and their wives, plus a hot peanut oil fryer. Even before I left for the family dinner, however, I was surprised by Helga's first phone call to me. She called to wish me a happy Thanksgiving even as she was cooking for her daughter and husband and their two young sons, plus Helga's two stepsons–whom she had taken in when her marriage had dissolved. Add to that dinner gathering a friend of the youngest stepson.

I earlier listed some of the attributes which attracted me to Helga. My comment about the "friend" brings into play an example of her being obedient to the Lord. Her youngest stepson, only nineteen at the time, had a friend who had just been released from a halfway house and had no place to stay. Bradley, the step-son, asked if his friend could stay with them for a while. Helga's selfless role in taking in a stranger in need was yet more assurance for me that she was indeed the loving Christian jewel I perceived her to be.

Helga's birthday was coming up and I gave her a letter over a Sunday lunch a few days before her actual birthday. Here are excerpts from that letter:

"Happy birthday, Helga! Knowing that you like to read I have chosen to give you an autographed copy of each of my three novels. Pardon my humility!

"I fully understand that you are still hurting from the devastating effects on your whole person as a result of your year-old divorce. I am both thrilled and deeply honored that I am allowed to call you my lady friend. Though to some it might seem premature for me to be so transparent—given that we have only known each other for a few weeks–but I feel you have been equally transparent with me.

"I have been drawn to your loveliness, to your sensitive and caring nature, and to the appeal of your desire to be obedient to our Father in heaven. I pray that each of us might, with time, discern God's will relative to growing our relationship.

"Lastly, know that you are in the Master Healer's hands for your own wounded heart. He wants you to be whole again, even as He is healing me. In loving thought, Terry."

A few days after that I received an e-mail from her. Here are excerpts: "Good Morning, Terry! I don't quite know how to explain it, but I feel very, very blessed that you have selected me to be your special lady friend. All I ever wanted in life was to be precious/special in someone else's life, and you have made me feel exactly that way. God bless you always, Helga."

Each of my children would initially react quite differently to Helga's and my growing relationship, particularly when I announced our engagement several months later. At that time Jason waved a green flag in that he said, "Whatever makes you happy , Dad!" Wendi wanted details. Not only that, she wanted some credit. Incredibly, she had actually met Helga nearly twenty years earlier when she worked as a "temp" for the same firm, office and person! That was the last time they had contact with one another but it was Wendi who remembered the event once she heard Helga's name. Nevertheless, she gets the yellow flag. As for Martin, he called for a full time-out. Red flag!

The final entry in my "Journey Alone" journal came on December 8, 2005. It began with: "Helga and I are in love. She told me the other day that the wall she had erected between herself and another relationship was crumbling like the Berlin Wall of 1990."

I concluded the entry with a comment that truly signaled the beginning of a new journey: "Seeing each other only on Sundays no longer meets either Helga's or my interests. We have decided to embark on a two-person Wednesday evening devotional series. We met for the first time for this purpose last evening at the church. The book I purchased for this study is entitled, *Devotions for Dating Couples: A Guide To Spiritual Intimacy*."

WITH A SONG IN MY HEART

Barely a month from when Helga and I first met, I asked her to meet me in our church's old sanctuary for our regular Wednesday evening devotional meeting. I walked her through the narthex and into the South campus sanctuary and asked her to sit on a stool near the dais. I could tell she was very nervous. In fact (I would later learn) she was praying I wasn't going to "surprise" her. As we walked through the door I tried to reassure her that this was no big deal, but I doubt she was much relieved. Once she was perched on the stool I proceeded with my plan, which was merely to sing two lines of a lively 1940's pop song whose beat I slowed enough to allow the few stanzas to come across as a ballad. The lyrics were these: "Who wouldn't love you, who wouldn't care? You're so enchanting, people must stare."

It was then, as I helped her off the stool and led her to a pew seat, that I said—softly and light-heartedly, although for the first time—"I love you." She was impressed with my singing effort, if not its quality, but was neither crying nor laughing. In fact, she was quite candid as she put her reaction up front by saying, "I'm not ready to say that to you."

Some would call that unrequited love, but what did she know? Heck, I hadn't planned to say that myself. All I wanted was to make an impression on her. Mission accomplished. Anyway, I had barely begun my campaign to capture her heart. But I *had* fired the first salvo. I felt the Lord had led me to her and I wasn't about to be weak-kneed about it!

From then on I filled up her dance card. Literally. Before many weeks had passed I had taken her to a play I had been wanting to see for nearly ten years but simply hadn't bothered. We played cards. I took her bowling and then dancing. I even signed us up for—and we took—several ballroom dancing lessons. I also quickly discovered that she could beat me at all of my own games! Was my male ego up to it? Absolutely, because there was an overarching lesson to everything we did together. We simply liked being with one another. And there was an incredible bonus for me. My special lady friend shared with me that she not only loved to cook and clean house, but liked to wash cars!

When I shared with her my enthusiasm for her enthusiasm, her sense of humor again showed off in her mock response. I would repeat a few of her exact words in conversation with every member of my family over the next month as well as loudly doing so at our family wedding reception . What was her line that had cracked me up? "Me strong German voman. Have baby in field and go back to work." No, we are *only* taking on grand babies.

I waited for nearly another two months before actually springing my proposal of marriage. For that I chose a regular Monday evening Stephen Ministry meeting. I covered up my secret by telling her Valorie had asked me to last-minute substitute for someone in delivering the evening's devotional. I found it a bit more difficult to explain why Mickey (from the church's technical department) was video-taping the procedure.

As I indirectly led up to my proposal-in-song—which was the first and last time I will ever solo sing in public—she whispered to someone sitting next to her, "What is he up to?" I had prepared my no-talent singing the best I could by enlisting a good friend and self-described song-and-dance man to coach me. Alas, he was working with clay diluted with far too much water. My disclaimer to the group of thirty Stephen Ministers just prior to launch was, "I have no talent for this, but I *do* have the guts to do it!"

At the end of my preliminary devotion I invited "my favorite Stephen Minister" to please come forward. By the way she carried herself up front I thought I saw a spark of deviousness in her eyes, but I had my own agenda to deal with, and I was very nervous.

Taking her hand I proceeded to sing my heart out, not with the mere two lines from before, understand, but the same song's seven lines ... with one customized final line. At that point I kept her hand but went to a kneeling position. I had a vague thought that she seemed to be tilting her head to one side. I had seen that before and I wasn't a bit comforted.

The full lyrics went as follows:

> Who wouldn't love you? Who wouldn't care?
> You're so enchanting, people must stare.
> You're the dream this dreamer dreams about.
> Who wouldn't love you? Who wouldn't buy,
> the west side of heaven, if you winked your eye?
> You're the answer to my fondest prayer, Darlin'.
> Who wouldn't love you? Who wouldn't care?
> Will you marry me, Helga? Please say you will.

I held that final note for several beats even though I knew I was flat. But I got through it and thought I was home. After I had been on my knees nearly a full minute, however, my hands still clasped in the air in front of her, I had still heard no response. Then I heard someone say, "She hasn't answered him!" Yup, she did it to me. After all my hard work and planning she was stringing me out! Finally, as I struggled to my feet she smiled and whispered, "I will."

REVELATION

Within a few days I made arrangements at the church for the wedding date to which we had tentatively agreed, May 6, four months hence. Man makes plans but God orders the steps. He had slightly different steps in mind.

We announced our intentions to our children and their spouses. Wendi, Martin and Tracie all expressed their preference that we wait a while and get to know one another better. We winked at each other as we tried to gently and tactfully explain what our minds and our hearts were telling us. After all, we were hardly the 18-to-20-year olds we were when we first made such decisions in life.

Early on we both felt strongly that our meeting was God-driven, so who were we to dispute His plan? We did carefully examine not only our individual walks with the Lord, but also our backgrounds, interests, personalities, and even our financial situations and philosophies in that regard. We knew what we knew, which was that we were not only compatible but equally yoked; spiritually, financially, and in terms of personality.

Everyone finally came around, but within weeks we dropped another bomb shell–a dramatic change in the wedding date! Here's what and how that developed. Helga had at first suggested an August wedding date. I had countered with May. She offered compromise with July. I held to May. Then she offered June, but I stubbornly clung to May. She finally agreed, but shortly after that things got wacky.

Within a few days of the first date's announcement Helga realized she was committed to a long-standing late May trip to Germany with her kids and grandchildren. She said to me, "I'm not going without you. We have to move up the wedding date!" At that I cracked up.

Revelation time. Until I wrote this book no one but Helga and I knew what I'm about to reveal. Before we ever announced our wedding date we actually discussed eloping. The idea behind it was merely a matter of keeping things simple and expeditious. The only thing that killed it was the fact that neither of owned the proper length ladder. I mean, isn't that what eloping couples do? The suitor hoists a ladder to his intended's bedroom window in order to steal her away, with the money-saving blessing of the families. Okay, so we fairly quickly wrote off Plan A.

Then, we much more seriously considered Plan B, which was to have a justice of the peace marry us, but without telling family. What? Sure. That way we could secretly live together as a married couple (going back and forth between our two homes, I guess), and then in May we would have a small family-only church wedding. We floated that hot-air balloon for nearly two days before it fell from a combination of leaking gas and excessive weight. We then settled for Plan C.

Neither of us wanted me to stay home with the dog while Helga and family went to Germany, so we would obviously have to go as a married couple. We could move up the wedding date a few weeks. Then, thinking it would take some time for our real estate agent to show us a house that perfectly met our needs, budget and hearts, we put both of our houses on the market and began looking for our own home.

The fourth house we looked at was a perfect match. Since you snooze, you lose, we made a late January offer that wouldn't fit with a May marriage. The upshot of all that dictated our moving up our wedding plans nearly two months, to March 11. I well remember my daughter's phrasing and tone over the telephone when I told her of the revised wedding date. "Moving up the wedding *two* months, huh?" I know she must have had her hand on her hip at the time.

While at Helga's house one evening in January 2006, after having helped her clean up the kitchen following a wonderful meal she had cooked for her family and me, she pulled her calendar and began checking dates that might meet our revised wedding plans. The young man she had taken into her home from a half way house several months earlier on behalf of her stepson's plea asked her what she was doing. Helga nonchalantly said, "I'm checking dates that will work for Terry and me to be married." His reaction was, "You're kidding!" I suspected then–and even now–that his reaction was born of an instant realization that his free bed and board was suddenly coming to an end.

BULLET SUMMARY

Early in life my parents put me in a place where I could learn about God, about my sin against Him, about His grace and forgiveness, about Christ's sacrifice on the cross, about his resurrection and triumph over both sin and death, about the way to salvation, and about His will for me. I didn't learn either those lessons, or the most important one of all, which is having a right relationship with Jesus Christ. As a consequence I wandered for forty years separated from God. Some of my lessons were learned in very difficult fashion, but not a one of them was meant for nothing.

I met my high school sweetheart, a wonderful Christian woman who was willing to marry me in spite of my lack of faith. We were unequally yoked only in that respect, however, and she prayed for me every day from when we first met. The lessons I had not learned when they were put before me in church–if not at home–cost Judy and me the opportunity to raise our three children in the Lord's ways. Judy salvaged some of that by keeping them always in her prayers, and through their early childhood by leading them in their own nightly prayers, even if they were mostly rote.

I learned about and endorsed evolution in college. And that very disregard for man's dependence upon God for life and living led to my passive acceptance of a pro-abortion stance without–and I now thank God–ever having been a party in our own lives to that particularly heinous sin. Bullets were flying all over the place and that I wasn't fatally struck—before God in His prevenient grace revealed Himself to me—was miraculous. But even though He preveniently comes to us, our response to His pursuing us must be to seek Him.

It seemed such a short time that our three children each finished their education, left the nest, found gainful employment, fell in love and happily married. I finally came to accept Christ as my Lord and Savior, and Judy and I retired from the industry which had kept us solvent for forty years. Alakazam and whammo. We went from marriage at age 20 to my accepting God's gift of salvation at age 58 to retirement from business at age 65, to the loss of the first love of my life at age 67. Before that latter event, things had seemed to be perfectly lined up for Judy and me in this earthly life.

I suspect that many reading this book have either been in a relatively similar situation as me at some point in life, or have friends or family members who have—that is, with respect to questioning one's faith, or the lack of it. We all have a tendency to think just because we make plans they'll happen the way we think or hope. The reality is that God does not guarantee even the next day. Therefore, to wait even a single day to embrace the Creator of the universe is sheer foolishness.

REJOICING IN THE NEW DAY

For those of us who have lost a mate, a parent, a child, or have suffered (or are suffering now) through some other life tragedy, it seems as if Winter will never end and Spring might skip its turn; that the tragic event in our lives is only an ending. But for the survivor, it must also be a beginning. One writer who lost his spouse put it this way: "I knew my life would never be the same again. But I didn't know that it could somehow, someway, still be okay." Healing transcends survival.

Though you may not share my Biblical belief in Christ Jesus as the savior of the world, I am yet humble enough to say I don't know how to convince you of that position . . . but I do know what Jesus has done for me. I have tried to describe those things. Out of them have come lessons in helping me grow through several seasons of change. When the Israelites described in the book of Exodus were wandering in the wilderness they often complained that God was far from them. The fact is that God was as close to them as their next breath, just as He has been for me.

We all need to take stock of what wonderful blessings we have enjoyed (and continue to enjoy) in life, the people whom we love and value tremendously, and also what is sacred to us. "Thank you, God, for allowing me to have had this time together with my loved ones." God has made a promise to us through Isaiah 41:10, one which I have taken to heart: "So do not fear, for I am with you; do not be dismayed, for I am your God. I will strengthen you and help you."

One of the things Judy said to me in her final week on this earth was this: "He gives us a new day."

Just as Jeremiah was called in the time of his Old Testament book to declare a "new day," all those who are adopted by God through the shed blood of Christ–the Messiah for Jews and Gentiles alike–are called to bring hope to our time.

Inspired by my beloved late wife, Judy, encouraged by my newly married and beloved wife, Helga, and founded in thankfulness for the grace of my own new days I continue my e-mail newsletter ministry–begun in the Fall of 2002. In November of 2006 I renamed it *New Day Newsletter*.

CLOSURE

It is quite apparent that God allows suffering in our lives, and for some He allows much more than others, but in no case are these tough lessons meant for nothing. On the contrary, these critical challenges are, indeed, lessons. If for no other reason, suffering serves to mitigate some of the pride in our lives, for you and I are obviously not in control. In John 15:2 God clearly tells us that He cuts off every branch in us that bears no fruit, while every branch that does bear fruit He prunes, so that it will be even more fruitful.

I think this is a remarkable verse that requires some maturity to fully understand. Martin Luther got it, albeit after much trial and error over many years. He welcomed such pruning, saying, "I am being fertilized, hoed, pruned and stripped of superfluous leaves; but I know the purpose well. The world is mistaken in its assumption that I shall die and perish. No, this is the work of my dear Father, who is cultivating the vine that it may grow well and have a good yield."

I recently read a book about God's grace by Steve McVey. He takes a position on the cliche that God won't put any burden on you greater than you can bear. He doesn't believe it, and neither do I. God *will* put heavier burdens on you than can bear. He certainly did with me. He allowed my burden to be greater than I could bear so that I would allow Him to bear it for me.

God's purpose in the breaking process was to bring me to the end of my own resources so that I was ready to understand that He is the only resource I need in life. Judy, for example, knew that her own abilities were not sufficient to rise to the challenge. She knew

He doesn't just *give* strength, He *is* our strength. This may sound as if it goes against what you believe, but God has no intention of helping us get stronger. He wants us to become so weak that *He* can express Himself as the strength you and I need in every situation.

What saved Judy at a tender age and brought her peace throughout her entire life was her trust in God. Through that trust she wanted to be obedient to Him and love both God and people. Thus was she saved by grace through faith, and not through her works. The curse (that is, the Law, because we could not keep it) which has rested on Man since Adam, was taken on by Jesus. Thus, neither Judy nor any one could boast of their own efforts to be saved, but only thank God by trusting in Him (see Galatians 3:10-13).

I have detailed the matter of my own wandering for forty years without Him, which I translate as having been spiritually lost. And look, if it could happen to Moses–someone God counted as righteous and thus saved long before Christ came to earth to bring us the message of the Gospels—it could certainly happen to you. Maybe it already has . . . or is.

The single most important aspect of my life–my coming to accept Jesus Christ as both my Lord and Savior through God's prevenient grace–came only at a time when I had finally come to the realization that something huge was terribly missing. Mine was a life that was otherwise happy and joyful with respect to Judy and our marriage, with respect to my family, and with respect to my work. Very simply, however, I did not know Jesus Christ.

As a result of that hole in my heart I had no way of producing fruit. The nearly eight full years following my surrender to Christ on Christmas Day in 1996 were by far the best years of Judy's and my lives together, even though all those years preceding them would surely have served to suit most of the 60% of marriages that today result in divorce.

The incredible blessings I have received in life through my two marriages, our children and grandchildren, and the times of our lives have been exactly that . . . blessings. I have also benefitted tremendously by letting myself be influenced by each of the two wives of my life.

There is one aspect of my life, however, that I never fully appreciated until I was nearly finished with writing this book. The impact of this aspect required more than 60 years to mature. First, indulge the reprinting of what I wrote in 1984, in the dedication of my first book:

"The industrialized world was yet again testing its ability to survive. In 1944, a small-town mother of three young boys struggled, waiting for her Marine husband to return from his nightmare in paradise. But their personal world war trial in the South Pacific wasn't enough. The eldest boy, barely seven years old, thrust his family into even deeper waters by dancing with an autumn leaf fire.

"The boy lay in his hospital bed, traumatized by third degree burns over nearly ten percent of his body. His upcoming year-long rehabilitation, including relearning how to walk, would be made possible in great part because of his mother's untrained but calm initial emergency response. Under the doctor's phone directions, she cut away all the burned and still-smoldering skin of her son's right leg. That effort and her subsequent tireless care guaranteed his complete recovery.

"After five separate skin-graft operations had been performed, the doctor explained that unless the parents were willing to regularly and progressively stretch their son's leg–to the point of blood spurting from the freshly grafted skin–he would be crippled for life. The father's emotion-numbing experience of hand-to-hand combat on the islands of Guam and Guadalcanal had fortunately (in an ironic twist) steeled him to meet the task. A part of the overall price, however, would be the family's endurance of the boy's cries of pain as the father executed the leg-strengthening regimen."

It has only now come to me that the childhood physical trials which nearly cost me my life were gain.

The same can be said for having totally lost any spiritual life between the ages of 18 and 58, as well as the wrenching emotional loss of my first wife. I have also lost one of my brothers and my father, as my mother yet clings to life by a thread. Yet, by the grace of God I have been blessed in so many ways. Alphonse Karr wrote, "Some people grumble because roses have thorns; I am thankful that thorns have roses." Who are we that God should grant us the blessings of our lives?

Consider our sad condition relative to our appreciation of the Maker. If we were to be rewarded with what we deserve we would have nothing. Not only are life's toughest lessons meant for something, they make our lives what they are. God prunes and refines us for our benefit and growth, although more often than not we simply don't understand it. Through God's pruning in my life I have been refined to produce far more fruit for His kingdom than I could possibly have produced without those trials. And I am certain He is not yet finished with me.

- End -